What
EXPERT
teachers do

What
EXPERT
teachers do

Enhancing professional knowledge
for classroom practice

JOHN LOUGHRAN

London and New York

First published in Australia by Allen & Unwin in 2010

This edition published in 2010
by Routledge
2 Park Square, Milton Park, Abingdon, Oxon, OX14 4RN
Simultaneously published in the USA and Canada
by Routledge
270 Madison Avenue, New York, NY 10016

British Library Cataloguing in Publication Data
A catalogue record for this book is available from the British Library

Library of Congress Cataloging-in-Publication Data
A catalogue record has been requested for this book

ISBN10:   0-415-57967-8 (pbk)
ISBN10:   0-203-85147-1 (ebk)

ISBN13:   978-0-415-57967-4 (pbk)
ISBN13:   978-0-203-85147-0 (ebk)

Typeset in 12/14.5pt Bembo by Post Pre-press Group, Australia
Printed and bound in Singapore by KHL Printing Co Pte Ltd

10 9 8 7 6 5 4 3 2 1

Contents

Tables and Figures   vii
Preface   ix
Acknowledgements   xiii

Part 1: Understanding Teaching and Learning

1   Thinking about teaching   3
2   Thinking about learning   20
3   Pedagogy   36

Part 2: Knowledge of Practice in Action

4   Prior knowledge   57
5   Processing   78
6   Linking   91
7   Translation   104
8   Synthesising   125
9   Metacognition   142

Part 3: Professional Learning

10   Growing professional knowledge through reflection   161
11   The value of teacher research   184
12   Developing knowledge of practice through
          professional learning   200

Conclusion   217

Bibliography   220
Index   227

Tables and Figures

Tables

Table 2.1 Deep and surface learning 30
Table 3.1 Content representation (CoRe) 46
Table 4.1 Know–What–Learn–How (KWLH) 71
Table 4.2 Anticipation reaction guide 73
Table 5.1 Question grid: Frogs 84
Table 5.2 Information grid 85
Table 5.3 Example of a 'chunking' grid 87
Table 5.4 Plus–Minus–Interesting (PMI) grid: Mummification 90
Table 6.1 From there to here: The Crusades 96
Table 9.1 Action and question stems 155
Table 12.1 Teacher and student views of teaching and learning 211

Figures

Figure 4.1 Probe of prior views 63
Figure 4.2 Reflective writing: Velcro 64
Figure 4.3 Reflective writing: The First Fleet 65
Figure 4.4 Card sort exercise 66
Figure 4.5 Concept map: Mount Vesuvius 68
Figure 4.6 Concept map: Trees 69
Figure 4.7 Concept map: Spiders 70
Figure 4.8 Semantic map: Ants 75
Figure 4.9 Frayer model: Vegetables 76
Figure 5.1 Jumbled text: Pyramids 83
Figure 5.2 Question dice 86
Figure 5.3 Fact file: Spiders 88
Figure 5.4 Writing on reading 89
Figure 6.1 A labelled diagram 97
Figure 6.2 The linking cycle 98
Figure 6.3 Mind map: Wool 103

Figure 7.1 Story from a graph   109
Figure 7.2 Slowmation: Pharaohs   115
Figure 7.3 Slowmation: Rowing   115
Figure 7.4 Fortune line: Marie Antoinette   117
Figure 7.5 Model making: Topography to contour   117
Figure 7.6 Velocity/time graph 1   121
Figure 7.7 Velocity/time graph 2   122
Figure 8.1 What can you work out?: Terra Australis   131
Figure 8.2 Before before, after after   133
Figure 9.1 Venn diagrams: Plants and animals   156
Figure 9.2 Moving-on map   157

Preface

There is a considerable literature describing the diversity of views on the nature of teachers' professional knowledge of practice. However, despite the wide range of these views, understanding what teachers' professional knowledge really is, what it looks like, and how it might be interpreted and implemented through classroom actions is exceptionally difficult. As teachers, we often struggle to define our knowledge because it is largely tacit. We are so busy teaching that there is little time, opportunity or expectation to talk about why we do things the way we do. Because our knowledge of our practice is tacit, it is often misunderstood despite the fact that it is fundamental to the quality of classroom teaching and learning.

To date, most of the writing about teachers' professional knowledge has been by academics for academics. There has not been a tradition of teachers talking about their knowledge of practice in quite the same way as that of some other professions. Teachers' professional knowledge of practice matters because:

- it is important to be able to recognise and articulate the expertise that is encompassed in high quality practice for ourselves and for the wider community;
- there is a continual need to communicate and share our knowledge of practice in ways that extend beyond tips and tricks as the sole measure or expectation of classroom expertise;
- we need to be reminded that the skills we develop in managing the dilemmas and tensions inherent in working with 25 or so different students each lesson is a basis for specialist knowledge;
- expertise needs to be able to be shared in ways that do not always call on each individual to reinvent the wheel; and
- teachers' professional knowledge encapsulates the essence of being an accomplished practitioner.

In the actions we take to facilitate student learning, we are continually developing our professional knowledge of practice. By valuing what we do, in accepting that good teaching requires skills, knowledge and abilities, it stands to reason that such knowledge needs to be recognised, developed and cultivated. Articulating our professional knowledge requires a shared language from which genuine meaning, application and value to our daily work as teachers might be derived.

As a high school English and History teacher, Joe Senese (2002) formulated three axioms that helped him to better understand his own practice. These were a way of capturing the essence of his knowledge of practice and helped him to think holistically about what he was doing, and how and why. They helped him to better direct the way his intentions for student learning played out in his teaching actions. His axioms were:

- Go slow to go fast.
- Be tight to be loose.
- Relinquish control in order to gain influence.

Senese described how, through choosing to look more deeply into his teaching, that which once appeared shapeless and chaotic actually contained patterns. In studying his own teaching he was able to tentatively generalise from his experiences in ways that allowed him to recognise and name those patterns. Each approach to naming communicated important perspectives about teaching.

Approaches to naming and framing a knowledge of practice through such things as axioms is not meant to be a blueprint or a recipe for practice, but rather a guide which, through appropriate reflection, might be interpreted, adjusted and adapted to suit the perceived needs of a given teaching and learning situation. Accomplished teachers' practice should be informed by their knowledge of teaching in ways that enhance the quality of their teaching and ultimately foster more meaningful student learning. It is not difficult to see that recognising, articulating and portraying teachers' knowledge of practice is central to better valuing teachers and teaching.

Structure of the book

The available knowledge on teaching and learning is immense. Many books are devoted to describing aspects of that literature in minute detail. However, as teachers, we are often so concerned with finding new teaching procedures and activities for the topics we are teaching that the available literature on teaching and learning is not an immediate port of call for informing our daily practice. Therefore, as a beginning point, Part 1 of this book is designed to act as a friendly reminder about some of the crucial underlying features and theories of teaching and learning that inform our practice. By briefly bringing together some of these features it is intended to demonstrate how such work helps to inform what we do and how skilled we are at managing teaching and learning. Part 1 then *builds up* from these teaching and learning ideas into notions of professional knowledge of practice, demonstrating that professional knowledge is something that extends beyond traditional academic texts.

Part 2 *builds out* from the foundations established in Part 1 and uses some 'big picture concepts' of teaching and learning to illustrate how a knowledge of practice might be framed. It illustrates what a language of professional knowledge might look like and, most importantly, how that knowledge is translated into practice through examples from real classrooms. Each of the chapters in Part 2 highlights knowledge of practice through the language being used to frame it and demonstrates the value and importance of that language through classroom examples of teaching. For example, the language of teaching and learning used to articulate knowledge of practice is demonstrated through the use of teaching procedures across a range of year levels and subject areas. In so doing, these examples of teaching procedures in a given context illustrate how a knowledge and language of practice can be used to both direct and inform teaching and learning. More so, they illustrate how accomplished teaching requires much more than just a range of teaching procedures; it is about why a teaching procedure is selected and how it is used for a particular reason that is purposefully linked to anticipated learning outcomes. These chapters highlight how professional knowledge goes beyond simplistic notions of using teaching procedures to simply break up the normal routine or for students to do fun activities. It is about engaging students in learning in ways that create a real need to know and a desire to accept greater responsibility for becoming active learners.

Part 3 concludes the book and places the ideas from the two preceding parts into the context of teachers' work. It challenges notions of professional development (typically seen as telling teachers what to do) and highlights the importance of professional learning (supporting teachers in directing their own knowledge growth). This section is designed to create real possibilities for the ongoing development of teachers' specialist knowledge and skills so that what it means to be an accomplished teacher is better able to be described, understood and valued.

Acknowledgements

To Airlie, Holly, Allister and Sophie for again supporting me in completing this book.

I am most grateful to Cate Baird, Liz Freer, Vojteck Markus, Bree Moody and Esther Rowe for so graciously sharing their work and their thinking about practice with me and allowing it to be reproduced in this book. Also, thanks to PEEL and SENSE Publishers for allowing reproduction of some of their publications.

A special thanks to Amanda Berry for her thoughtful comments and careful proofreading of the final manuscript.

Part 1
Understanding Teaching and Learning

Part 1 of this book introduces ideas about teaching and learning that are designed to illustrate the importance of seeing both as complex and interwoven. Although it is important to be technically competent, as teachers we need to be able to move beyond this form of competence alone. There is a clear need for us to continue our development in ways that encourage us to see more deeply into the complex nature of teaching and learning. In seeing into teaching and learning from different perspectives, the importance of the relationship between teaching and learning stands out, and it is in this relationship that real understanding of pedagogy emerges—that is where our expertise resides. Expert pedagogues understand the relationship between teaching and learning in ways that inform their practice and enhance not only their students' learning but also the growth of their own professional knowledge of practice.

1
Thinking about teaching

There are many skills in teaching that, when combined, form an important base from which initial teaching competence may be derived. Most of these skills require refinement and development over time because, in many instances, they are not a part of our normal patterns of behaviour. Therefore, as teachers, we need to make a conscious effort to pay attention to these skills to ensure that what we think we do in our practice is in accord with what we actually do, and that is not a simple task.

Some of these skills appear to be quite obvious, but there is a noticeable difference between being aware of certain behaviours and purposefully enacting them in our practice. That becomes even more difficult when the skills run counter to our normal behaviours. Therefore, as a starting point in thinking about our teaching, it is important to become a keen observer of our own behaviours, as well as the behaviours of others, in order to consciously develop strategies and approaches to teaching that will be conducive to high quality learning.

At the simplest level, such things as rhetorical questions, talking over others, put-downs (inadvertent or otherwise), ignoring and many other behaviours that we all display from time to time can become serious barriers to students' open and honest engagement in classroom learning. Paying attention to such things in our own patterns of behaviour is important because the ability to moderate or change such behaviours requires ongoing effort and attention. In addition, recognising and responding to students' behaviours is also essential because these behaviours are equally important in shaping the nature of the teaching and learning environment.

The following section briefly considers some of the technical skills of teaching that form a base for practice and also highlights how moving beyond skills alone matters in developing expertise in teaching.

Questioning

Questioning is a most important teaching skill that comprises many different components such as:

- question frequency;
- question distribution;
- how responses to questions are dealt with (by teachers and students);
- individual/group directed questions;
- teacher/student generated questions;
- question types (for example, open/closed; factual/thinking; convergent/divergent; evaluative; higher-order); and
- questioning techniques (for example, Socratic).

Clearly, the list of aspects of questioning is extensive and varies depending on how the list is categorised. However, as demonstrated by those components briefly noted above, that which may at first glance appear simple and obvious is much more complicated and demanding when considered more deeply, and from varying perspectives.

Each of the points above impact teaching and learning differently depending on who is doing the asking (the teacher, an individual student, a group of students) and the level of importance perceived to be attached to the question and answer. The level of confidence, knowledge and ability of the questioner and answerer also need to be considered. For example, how you respond to a thoughtful question from a normally quiet student may be very different from your standard response to a commonly inquisitive or talkative student. You may be taken by surprise by the question from a quiet student and therefore respond in a more conscious and knowing way than the automatic response evoked by a much more talkative student. Being aware of what we are doing is important in order to seriously monitor and adjust our own teaching behaviours. There is a major difference between knowing and doing and, in our daily work as teachers, we are continually making decisions about how to act, when and why, in our interactions with our students. Such decisions are often subconscious and over time become routinised. However, the nature of our decisions matters because so much of what we do directly influences our students' learning.

For each of the categories of questioning noted above there are a range of skills that, when refined, make an enormous difference to the nature of our classroom interactions: teacher to student(s); student(s) to teacher; student(s) to student(s). Consider, for example, the frequency of questions. On the one hand, we can ask questions with such rapidity that answers are barely required, much less seriously valued. In such a situation our students soon learn how to respond and how much effort to put into their thinking. On the other hand, less frequent but more incisive questioning can demand very different behaviour from the same students. Of course the context also influences the underlying purpose of our actions and so what happens and why is not always for the same reason. However, as alluded to earlier, if our normal behaviour revolves around asking lots of questions then it can be very difficult to change that behaviour—it happens subconsciously or automatically. Therefore, despite *knowing* about questioning, thoughtfully applying that knowledge may not naturally follow in the *doing* of questioning. That is one reason why technical competence, or accumulating the base skills of teaching, in itself is not sufficient. Expertise is derived from purposely moving beyond knowing and into learning about consciously doing and doing with reason.

It seems obvious that if we ask a question and then respond positively only to those answers that are correct, then any of our students who are unsure or have different answers or want to ask a question in return will be less likely to engage in the process. We have all experienced at some time in our student career that embarrassing feeling of answering a question the wrong way and feeling foolish. Yet the skilled teacher knows how to avoid this situation by actively working to ensure that students honestly speak up and say what they think. The way an expert teacher reacts in such a situation may not be immediately noticeable to the casual observer because of the subtle aspects that make a difference and that do not necessarily stand out as being so dramatically different as to draw attention. When we respond to students by saying, 'Yes, that's right' or 'No, you're wrong', the language shapes our students' expectations of how to act. Because those responses may be part of our normal language, then, without realising it or meaning it, our normal behaviour can limit our students' willingness to contribute. It can also be very hard to see this in our own teaching but be immediately obvious in someone else's.

Compare the situation above to when we are conscious and careful about how to respond to our students. When we work to withhold judgement our students are encouraged to contribute in ways that are not possible when they think that only the right answer is acceptable. We can do this in lots of different ways, for example by using phrases such as 'Thanks for that, anyone else?' or 'Yes, that's an interesting point' or 'I hadn't thought of it that way myself, good thinking' or 'Does anyone have a different idea?' and so on. Through being conscious of how to respond to students, our normal behaviours can be modified so that there are fewer impediments to students' involvement in classroom discussion. The value of adjusting behaviours in this way can be further enhanced by allowing more students to respond before offering any comments or attempting to bring closure to the situation. Again, these simple changes in patterns of dialogue can have a dramatic influence on our classroom interactions, but they can be surprisingly difficult to implement because they are not the normal way we act.

It has been said many times that teaching is the only job where people ask questions about things to which they already know the answer. It is in this familiar pattern that the game of 'guess what's in the teacher's head' becomes ritualised. Unfortunately, despite experiencing that game as students ourselves, it is amazing how frequently teachers end up playing the same game in their own classrooms. As the discussion above highlights, being conscious of our own actions and how they are interpreted by others (students) is crucial to knowing and doing being more tightly aligned in practice.

Last century, Dan Lortie (1975) coined the phrase the *apprenticeship of observation* to describe how, through their years of schooling, students become accomplished observers of teaching. Yet, as Lortie noted, although students have seen lots of teachers teaching, they have actually only viewed teaching as a one-way process. They did not usually have access to the thinking and planning that underpinned their teachers' practice; what they saw was largely interpreted as teachers telling or imparting information. Therefore, it is easy for us to inadvertently and subconsciously apply an approach to teaching that has been shaped by being an observer of teaching from one side of the desk. As students we did not necessarily pay serious attention to what underpinned what was happening and why, so in moving to the other side of the desk we can sometimes act from these superficial understandings of practice shaped by our apprenticeship of observation.

If we do not pay enough attention to how to develop and enhance our skills, knowledge and ability as teachers, our apprenticeship of observation, our default behaviours and the subtleties of practice can conspire to confuse understanding the technicalities of teaching and gaining the knowledge that underpins genuine expertise. For example, as a knowledge of questioning is developed, a false sense of confidence can emerge that undermines a recognition of the value and purpose in moving beyond these skills alone. This is partly because knowing and doing are not always recognised as different in our own actions (despite often easily seeing the difference in others) and partly because understanding the difference really requires us to look more deeply into our actions and to question what we take for granted. It is much easier to rationalise our behaviour and justify particular actions than it is to genuinely reflect on what is happening, how and why (Loughran, 2002). It can also be very difficult to see the things that are closest to us; we need some distance to be able to see more clearly, to be adept at creating different vantage points from which to see ourselves in action. This notion of seeing from different perspectives is what Schön (1983) described as *reframing*. Reframing is crucial to questioning what we take for granted in our practice and encouraging us to reach out beyond the technical to develop genuine expertise.

Moving beyond the technical: Wait time

There is a well-known body of research conducted in the mid 1970s and early 1980s into aspects of *wait time* (Fagan, Hassler & Szabo, 1981; Rowe, 1974a, 1974b; Tobin & Capie, 1980). Wait time is that period of teacher silence that follows the posing of a question (wait time I) as well as the corresponding period of time following an initial student response (wait time II). In an initial study Mary Budd Rowe (1974a) analysed over 300 tape recordings of classroom teachers and discovered a mean wait time I of one second and a mean wait time II of 0.9 seconds.

Her findings were interesting for many reasons but perhaps the most pertinent is that she had empirical evidence to support the assertion that when teachers ask a question, their wait time is so short that students do not really have sufficient thinking time to formulate a well-reasoned response. For most teachers this result is easy to explain because, despite the demonstrated short wait time in the study, our experience tells us that an answer is already forming in our students' minds before we have finished asking the question, or that we are already looking around the classroom for likely respondents while we are asking the question. Therefore, we can easily justify a short wait time and in so doing, minimise the importance of that knowledge in *our own* practice. So an immediate problem is evident. Knowledge of wait time alone is not sufficient to change our normal wait time behaviour. Further to this, even when we acknowledge the importance of wait time we do not see that a lack of wait time exists in *our own* teaching; that is, it exists out there in other teachers' practice but not in our own. Thus there is an inherent contradiction between our knowing and our doing. So how do we bridge that gap?

Rowe's initial empirical results led to interesting research outcomes associated with the impact that changes in wait time can have when teachers provide at least three seconds of silent wait time after posing a question and similarly after a student response—doing so promotes learning as students have time to think about, reflect on and recall relevant prior knowledge. Increasing wait time encourages more thoughtful responses to the questions asked. Results showed that if the average wait time (both I and II) is extended beyond three seconds other improvements flow, which include:

- increased length of student responses;
- more frequent student contributions;
- increased logic of students' explanations;
- an increase in the use of evidence to support inferences;
- an increase in the frequency of speculative responses;
- an increase in the number of student questions; and
- an increase in participation from more reluctant learners.

One obvious conclusion is that teachers, regardless of the teaching environment, should increase their wait time and decrease their air time. When this happens and it is consciously applied it has been found that teachers:

- increase their use of higher-level evaluative questions;
- decrease the percentage of teacher talk; and
- become more flexible in their responses.

Therefore, *if* wait time knowledge is directly and purposefully applied in practice, real changes in students' learning can occur because real changes in teachers' behaviour is initiated.

This brief consideration of wait time illustrates how that which initially may appear simple and obvious is really much more complex and, when it comes to considerations of teaching, *the simple is complex* could well be regarded as a truism. So how do we make changes in our practice so that what we know and what we do can be more closely aligned?

Stephen Brookfield (1995), in his book *Becoming a critically reflective teacher*, introduces the notion of *assumption hunting*. By studying our own practice, good ideas and clearer understandings of classroom events are often recognised. This allows us to gain increased professional satisfaction through the process of sharing our new insights, which also encourages us to check our assumptions.

The literature suggests that when teachers do engage in such assumption-hunting activities they come to see a need to reframe their existing ideas, and their personal learning is significantly challenged as a consequence of viewing their actions from another perspective. Such assumption hunting and reframing works best when the investigation is collaborative because, through interaction with colleagues, the taken-for-granted ideas that we subconsciously hold can be challenged in positive ways through the eyes of a valued other. Typically, this process leads to the development of new knowledge and understanding about classrooms, teaching and learning. And herein lies the complexity of teaching. The knowledge about such things as questioning and wait time, at first glance, may appear simple, obvious and logical. However, putting that knowledge into practice in ways that truly enhance the nature of student learning requires different skills and abilities that, to the casual observer, may not be immediately discernible.

From a teacher's perspective, making good use of knowledge of practice is an idiosyncratic and personal endeavour that can be neither mandated nor easily measured. It requires a personal commitment to improvement that is largely based on intrinsic motivation. Success in recognising and changing personal behaviours involves taking the risk of looking at oneself with a critical eye and choosing to do something about it. It is neither easy to see nor to change one's practice as it depends on understanding that teaching is more than telling and that learning is more than listening.

Despite our best intentions, the apprenticeship of observation may well have had a greater impact on our practice than we might be prepared to acknowledge. Challenging our assumptions and learning how to make knowledge of practice meaningful in our teaching takes effort. Just as students need to develop as active and responsible learners, so too learning about teaching is equally demanding.

The following anecdote demonstrates how one student teacher chose to risk learning about wait time in his own practice and the value of that experience for his own professional learning.

Wait time

My first class. Palms sweating, breathing shallow, tie too tight, pulse too fast. I guess I was kind of nervous. I had fully prepared the whole lesson in intricate detail, and even rehearsed certain key sections. I shuffled my books, watching them enter the room noisily, with attitude to burn. They sat down. Eventually, I swallowed.

'Good morning 10B! My name is Mr Burns, I'm a teacher from Monash University. Today we are . . .' and into the lesson I launched. Cool as a cucumber and smooth as a strawberry smoothie. I wrote on the board in big letters: 'What Makes A Film?'

Having bonded with the students on an incredibly deep and substantial level in the first three minutes of the class, I swiftly and confidently turned to face the class. With a big smile and the most open of expressions I could muster, I threw out my first question.

'Can anyone tell me some elements of film making?'

I paused for the expected barrage of excited responses. I waited and waited. Anyone? Longer and longer. Help? It felt like an hour. A week. A year. Would the wait be worth it? Ah . . . yes? Finally from the back of the class! 'Um . . . scripts, sir?'

'Thank you!' I said, hopefully without too much desperation. The trickle of answers gradually became a waterfall. I was finally safe, splashing gleefully in the puddles of their intuitive responses, the dam of silence broken. (Loughran, 2002: 37)

Whether a student teacher or an experienced teacher, the same approach to risk taking applies. Learning about practice *through* practice is crucial for the development of expertise. Just as students need to accept responsibility for their own learning, so too as teachers we need to do the same. This is possible when we place ourselves in positions through which our experiences of doing things differently lead us to challenge and confront our taken-for-granted assumptions and behaviours. Through that process, new insights emerge and expertise of practice is purposefully developed.

Decision-making and teacher thinking

Teaching involves decision-making that occurs across a range of ideas, issues and events. In teaching, we need to make decisions about such things as:

- content (breadth and depth);
- student behaviour;

- the appropriate balance between teacher-directed and student-initiated tasks;
- expectations for student progress;
- homework;
- how to cater for different learning styles;
- personal philosophy of teaching and learning;
- teaching procedures; and
- assessment.

We do not all think the same way about the same things and we do not all think about the same things (some things matter more to some than others). Our individual experiences shape our understanding of the teaching role and how it should be played out in practice. Our own personal perspectives on all or any of the issues noted above shape not only what we do and how we do it but also the choices we make and why. We all have beliefs about the nature of knowledge and how students do and/or should acquire it. Our beliefs are dramatically influenced by our (often hidden) assumptions about the nature of teaching and how students learn. More so, we all have personal values that influence how we run our classrooms, what matters to us in terms of classroom management, respect, academic standards, self-esteem, etc.

Therefore, any circumstance that challenges, whether explicitly or implicitly, our views, ideas or philosophies will naturally prompt us to think about the situation in light of our own experiences and to consider the possibilities for action in relation to the competing demands inherent in the situation. On the one hand, there is the thinking and decision-making processes associated with planning the curriculum, a unit of work, or a lesson. On the other hand, there are the more immediate demands of decision-making associated with doing teaching such that choices about action are an ever-present and unavoidable aspect of practice. Therefore, although it is not easily seen and certainly difficult to capture, how we think as teachers is important in shaping how we act. Again, the apprenticeship of observation raises interesting issues about teacher thinking and decision-making. Because it is not easily seen, the principles that underpin teachers' thinking as well as the complexity of that thinking may be overlooked.

In many ways, if little attention is paid to teacher thinking then much of that practice will remain tacit, elusive and difficult to define. If that is the case then some of the most important knowledge that shapes practice could be dismissed or ignored, thus reducing the possibilities for understanding expertise in teaching. For some, this problem is associated with that which has come to be described as the *theory–practice gap* (Korthagen et al., 2001).

The idea of a theory–practice gap has limitations because it sets the two constructs as opposites, with unfortunate implications. At one extreme, knowledge of teaching, or theory, is seen as far removed from the real world of practice, while at the other extreme teaching is interpreted as only being about doing and as such has sometimes been described as atheoretical. The reality though is that teaching expertise involves theory in practice but the tacit nature of the underlying knowledge of teaching tends to mask its importance and limit the ways in which we are able to share that knowledge with one another. Therefore, arguments about a theory–practice gap tend to be reinforced when in fact it is as much about the limitations of language and forms of communication as it is about extreme differences between theory and practice. One way of reconceptualising this situation is through understanding teaching as being problematic.

Teaching is problematic

As the previous section suggests, there is not just one way of doing teaching. Because teaching comprises so many competing demands, these choices make teaching itself problematic. However, problematic should not be viewed in a negative sense. Understanding teaching as problematic means that teaching is dilemma based and, because by definition dilemmas are situations that need to be managed (not necessarily solved), it means that we are continually making judgements about what we consider to be appropriate actions in a given situation at a given time. That does not mean that the same action would lead to the same result in a different context or at another time, or that another teacher should do the same thing when confronted by a similar situation. Rather, it means that our personal professional judgement is paramount in responding to our students' needs and concerns—and that is why understanding teaching as problematic matters.

Coming to understand that there is not one correct and best way of doing teaching is embedded in experience: 'I can see important changes that have occurred in my practice as a result of confronting the gaps between my rhetoric and the reality of my teaching . . . The process of coming to terms with teaching dilemmas is, of course, neverending' (Zeichner, 1995: 20). As a beginning teacher, it can be quite common to seek 'the answers' about what to do and the best way to do it. That is only natural. But as familiarity with the process of teaching develops, as confidence in one's ability to manage grows, as the diversity of learners' needs and approaches to learning become increasingly apparent, seeing teaching as problematic rather than rule driven is almost inevitable. In coming to that realisation it also becomes increasingly clear that it is through reflecting on our decisions and professional judgements about our practice that our knowledge of teaching grows. As a consequence, it is not difficult to see how developing expertise in teaching is itself an educative process.

As the apprenticeship of observation suggests, at first glance teaching can appear to be an orderly process based on technical proficiency. However, when viewed from an experienced teacher's vantage point the constant undercurrent of choices, decisions, competing concerns, dilemmas and tensions become much more important in shaping what happens, how and why. For some this can be unsettling because it can mean that, despite all of the planning and preparation for teaching, there are still things that can happen that are not able to be anticipated; and that can lead to anxiety and unease in the practice setting. Donald Schön (1983) described teaching as an 'indeterminate swampy zone' and the reality is that teaching is 'a complex and messy terrain, often difficult to [map and] describe' (Berry, 2004: 1312). That is not a bad thing. It is just that teaching is not as smooth and straightforward as it may at first appear and becoming comfortable with that is part of what it means to understand teaching as being problematic.

If teaching is understood as problematic then it stands to reason that one aspect of learning about teaching is embedded in the journey

of development and growth is governed and directed by what individuals see as important to their practice through their experiences.
As Myers and Simpson note,

> teacher learning and professional practice fit better the idea of
> teaching as a never-ending process of investigating and experiment-
> ing, reflecting and analysing what one does in the classroom and
> school, formulating one's own personal professional theories and
> using these theories to guide future practice, and deciding what and
> how to teach based on one's best personal professional judgment.
> (1998: 58)

Therefore, part of that professional learning must involve discovering
new ways of seeing situations, testing out alternative approaches and
learning to see practice from not only a teacher's but also a learner's
perspective.

Because of the 'messiness of teaching' and the importance of
individuals accepting responsibility for directing their own professional learning, for some the desire for a much simpler solution is
strong because of the need to feel in control rather than be confronted by a sense of uncertainty. However, managing the desire to
seek a simple solution matters because it is through being challenged
by, and engaged in, mapping the indeterminate swampy terrain that
professional learning abounds. It is in accepting that teaching is problematic, and working with that conceptualisation, that we learn how
to adapt, adjust and construct our practice.

Understanding teaching as problematic is made all the more
obvious through what John Mason (2002) describes as *noticing*. Mason
suggests that a teaching situation is not really seen until it is seen differently. He argues that despite the superficial views of teaching that
are often put forward, teaching is rarely the same thing.

> At the heart of all practice lies noticing: noticing an opportunity
> to act appropriately. To notice an opportunity to act requires three
> things: being present and sensitive to the moment, having reason
> to act, and having a different act come to mind. Consequently,
> one important aspect of being professional is noticing possible acts

to try out in the future . . . A second important aspect is working on becoming more articulate and more precise about reasons for acting. The mark of an expert is that they are sensitised to notice things which novices overlook. They have finer discernment. They make things look easy, because they have a refined sensitivity to professional situations and a rich collection of responses on which to draw. Among other things, experts are aware of their actions. (Mason, 2002: 1)

As Mason notes, experts 'make things look easy' and, because some aspects of teaching look easy, expertise in teaching is often misunderstood. When teaching looks easy, the problematic is not so obvious, the uncertainty of practice is not so apparent and so what others notice and interpret is very different to what the teacher knows and feels when teaching. This point is demonstrated in the following account by Esther Rowe.

Letting go

Walking into the lab I was feeling confident that today's lesson was going to be different and the girls were going to like it. No notes today (at least not written by me). Today I was going to stand back and let the girls take control. We were starting our new topic, *Mixtures*, and as the girls got settled I said:

'Ok ladies today you are going to teach each other. In groups of four you are going to take one of the sub-topics from the board, research it and then present it to the class.'

Think Pair Share
As I was going through exactly how a Think Pair Share works, the hands started to go up.

'Can we pick our own groups?'

'Are we going to get marked on this?'

'Are we presenting them today?'

Not the response I was looking for. Since beginning teaching this year I have gotten into a routine of real 'chalk and talk' type lessons. Although the learning styles of some students are suited to this type of teaching, I wanted to take the focus of our lessons off me, my notes and my structured discussions and start to challenge my students' ideas about learning.

So these questions weren't helping me feel confident about changing the focus of my lessons.

'Hands down! You can ask questions later,' I said and as today was the day I was passing the control of the lesson over to my girls, I let them pick their own groups.

'Yes!!' I heard them whisper. Down went my confidence again. But as I watched them in their pairs I was pleasantly surprised. Almost everyone appeared to be on task.

'Five more minutes and then it's time to discuss in your group of four,' I instructed confidently.

Wandering around the room
As I wandered the room, I fought my natural urge to interrupt their discussions and steer their thoughts in a more productive direction but I did ask one group:

'How's it going? Are you enjoying this activity more than our usual science classes?'

'Yeah, this is so much better,' was the overwhelming response. 'Wow! That's exactly the response I was after,' I thought to myself, trying not to feel too crushed about what it meant about my 'normal' lessons. 'Maybe this is working. The girls are taking some control over their own learning and they are enjoying it. I'll give them a little more time, then it's back to the centre and away they'll go with their presentations.' The first group got up and without any prompting they began their presentation. 'Not bad,' I thought to myself. Then the next group and then the next. Before I knew it they had all done their presentations.

During the presentations
As their classmates were presenting, the girls were attentive and to my surprise writing notes as they went. 'So they don't need me writing endless notes on the board,' I thought to myself. Even more surprising was that every girl had a go at presenting. I was sure that a few of the quieter, less confident girls would try and get out of having a go.

It had all gone rather well, we had covered a lot of content and the girls seemed to really enjoy the different approach to the lesson. Up went a hand.

'Are we having a test on this stuff?'

'Yes, but not for a while. Don't worry about that now though please.'

'Will you give us proper notes for this stuff though?'

'What? You've got good notes,' I thought. Apparently if the notes are not from me they are not 'proper notes'. At this point I realised some of the girls had missed the point. They were totally capable of taking control of their own learning. They had just been doing it. I had seen it for myself. These girls, and so many others like them at our school, are spoon fed information and didn't think they had accomplished anything unless they had pages of writing to prove it.

'Am I going to be able to change their thinking overnight?' I thought to myself. 'No way. Could I chip away at it using activities such as this one to try and make them see their learning from a different angle? Sure!' I told myself with a sense of satisfaction and confidence.

In future . . .

I know I am not always going to have the time to give the girls control like I did in this situation. The bottom line is we've all got deadlines to meet, curriculum to follow and balancing all the demands is not easy. Sometimes there simply aren't enough days in the week to be able to do a hundred fabulous activities where the girls are able to challenge their ideas about their learning. However, I've demonstrated to myself that I am capable of 'letting go' and giving them a bit of freedom. And on most accounts it was a worthwhile thing to do. Although the girls may not have seen the benefits immediately like I did, it had been a positive learning experience; for both myself and the girls.

'Now to get them to see it more themselves. That's what I need to do. Yep, I'm not the only one who has to learn to let go.' (Rowe, 2008: 93–5)

Cases (see Shulman, 1992 for more on the cases methodology) such as Rowe's above are structured around the tensions and dilemmas that teachers experience in their own teaching. As the example above demonstrates, questioning the taken-for-granted revealed the complexities of teaching and learning in new ways. Through experimenting with her practice and subsequently writing an account of that experience, Esther Rowe illustrated exactly what John Mason was arguing for through his idea of noticing. In articulating aspects of the problematic nature of teaching she gained insights into her teaching and her students' learning. In so doing, she demonstrated how teachers' professional knowledge of practice is able to be captured, developed and portrayed.

Overview

This chapter on thinking about teaching has been organised in such a way as to make clear that expertise in teaching involves much more than the simple accumulation of technical skills, tips and tricks about how teaching is done. Although technical competence is an important base from which expertise in teaching grows, it is important to recognise that teaching is an educative process for both students and teachers.

Although to some, teaching may look easy, the reality is that it is a complicated and complex process, largely because it is problematic. The problematic nature of teaching means that the how and why of teachers' professional judgements matter and those judgements form the foundations for their understanding, development and use of knowledge of practice.

2
Thinking about learning

Jean Piaget was a psychologist whose research into children's cognitive development has been influential in education. His work is characterised by a sequence of four distinct developmental stages ranging from birth through to adulthood, each stage being a particular step in developmental progress (Piaget, 1953).

The first of Piaget's stages is *sensorimotor* (zero to two years). This stage includes the development of such things as simple reflexes (for example, sucking), first habits and object permanence; intentional actions (for example, shaking a rattle, doing things that are directed towards a goal such as seeking attention); and copying actions, speech and facial expressions.

The second stage is *preoperational* (two to seven years). This stage includes the development of symbolic thought and language through the use of gestures, and development of language and motor skills. In this stage, children are egocentric—they see things only from their perspective.

The third stage is *concrete operational* (seven to twelve years). This stage includes logical thinking, conservation and a shift away from egocentricism to an ability to see other perspectives.

The fourth and final stage is *formal operational* (twelve years to adulthood). This stage includes the capacity to think beyond concrete realities and to develop abstract possibilities.

The implications of Piaget's work can be viewed in two ways. The first is in accord with his theory that developmental processes occur in steps and that achievement is limited by a child's particular stage of development. A consequence of that view is that there is little point in trying to teach students skills until they reach the stage at which attaining that skill is deemed to be possible. The alternative perspective is based on a broad set of evidence that suggests 'so long as necessary prerequisite skills are either available to a child or can be taught, there is no fundamental reason . . . why a child cannot learn those abilities which Piaget considered to denote a higher stage of mental development' (Howe, 1999: 21).

Piaget's work was based on studying the individual and how that individual's cognitive development progressed. With such a focus on the individual it could be argued that Piaget ignored other influences that may be equally important in learning. For example, the Russian psychologist Lev Vygotsky proposed a different way of thinking about cognitive development that contrasted to Piaget's view.

Vygotsky described learning as occurring in a social context and so his ideas about sociocultural and sociohistorical influences on cognitive development offered a different perspective on the development of learning; his view was that learning was culturally mediated. As a consequence, Vygotsky suggested that children's development of specific knowledge represents the shared knowledge of a particular culture. Vygotsky argued that children attained that knowledge through a process of internalisation (Vygotsky, 1962).

Vygotsky described mental ability as comprising two distinct functions: lower mental functions (those things that are inherited), which are controlled by external events; and higher mental functions (developed through social interaction), which are controlled internally (thinking, abstraction and language, for example).

Vygotsky also introduced the idea of a *zone of proximal development* (ZPD), which can be characterised as 'the distance between what children can do by themselves and what they can do with others' (Krause, Bochner & Duchesne, 2003: 63). In essence, the ZPD is about the difference between what children are able to do with some assistance as opposed to what they are able to do unassisted. The extent of that difference is their ZPD and it is not the same for all children, or for all children of the same age.

The difference then between Piaget's and Vygotsky's theories in terms of implications for learning is interesting. On a strict interpretation of Piagetian theory, learning is limited by the developmental stage that a student occupies, whereas Vygotsky's focus on the social nature of learning suggests that social, cultural and historical experiences have a big part to play in a student's cognitive development.

Piaget's and Vygotsky's research has had an enduring influence on education, not so much because of their theories per se but because their approach to researching learning highlighted the value of observation. Their work helps to focus more attention on the need for our professional judgements as teachers to be informed by our efforts to better match expectations of cognitive development with the myriad social and physical factors that might support the learning process in appropriate ways for different children in different ways in the same classroom.

Intelligence

The notion of intelligence is a much contested field as is illustrated by the nature–nurture debate—whether intelligence is a result of genetic inheritance or environmental influence. As is so often the case, the use of a dichotomy leads to polarisation because of the either/or choice. It is hard to imagine that intelligence is either fully inherited or solely shaped by environmental factors, since clearly both have an influence. However, allocating the definitive position on the continuum is no easy task; a task exacerbated by the obvious differences in individuals.

The idea that intelligence underpins what we are able to do may seem reasonable enough, but difficulties arise when attempting to determine what the list of capabilities central to intelligence actually comprises. These difficulties are particularly apparent when it comes to measuring intelligence and are highlighted through the debates surrounding IQ (Intelligence Quotient) tests.

Originally, IQ tests were designed by psychometricians as an attempt to measure children's everyday, commonsense knowledge. The early tests, Binet's IQ tests, were expressed as a percentage of mental age divided by chronological age, and they were later refined for use with adults (Weschler Intelligence Scales). However, as suggested above, that which comprises intelligence has a big influence on that which is measured. By the time sociocultural factors and other contextual influences on testing were factored in, IQ as a precise measure of intelligence became hotly contested.

It was partly as a consequence of the ways in which IQ was being conceptualised, understood and used that led Howard Gardner to propose his theory of *multiple intelligences*, which stands in stark contrast to the notion of one measure to represent general cognitive ability. In fact what Gardner and many other psychologists have done through their theories of intelligence is to facilitate a shift away from some form of general mental capability alone and to illustrate how intelligence can vary depending on the nature of the task, the context, level of motivation, and so on.

Gardner's theory of multiple intelligences was first laid out in his book *Frames of mind: The theory of multiple intelligences* (1983). He initially proposed seven intelligences (which later grew to eight and recently there has been some consideration of a ninth) and suggested that these intelligences rarely operated independently of one another—they were used at the same time (to varying degrees) and in a complementary fashion. His categories include:

- *bodily kinaesthetic intelligence*: the use of mental abilities to coordinate bodily movements;
- *interpersonal intelligence*: the ability to understand the intentions and motivations of others;
- *verbal linguistic intelligence*: the ability to learn languages, and to use language to accomplish certain goals;
- *logical mathematical intelligence*: the ability to analyse problems, mathematical operations, and to investigate scientifically;
- *naturalistic intelligence*: the ability to recognise, categorise and draw upon certain features of the environment;
- *intrapersonal intelligence*: the ability to understand oneself—feelings, fears and motivations;
- *visual spatial intelligence*: the ability to recognise and use the patterns of a space; and
- *musical intelligence*: the ability to recognise and compose musical pitch, tone and rhythm.

Gardner's theory of multiple intelligences has had a major impact on thinking about learning in schools. Interestingly, although his work has been embraced in the education community, it has not been so readily accepted in psychology.

Building on this notion of different intelligences, Daniel Goleman's *Emotional intelligence* (1996) further pushes the boundaries of what comprises intelligence and highlights the difficulties of attempting to define intelligence through one numerical measure. Briefly, Goleman suggests that emotional intelligence comprises:

- *self-awareness*: the ability to read one's emotions;
- *self-management*: the ability to control one's emotions;
- *social awareness*: the ability to react to others' emotions; and
- *relationship management*: the ability to develop others while managing conflict.

Another view of intelligence is the *triarchic model* of intelligence proposed by Robert Sternberg (1985). This model is another example of the rejection of the notion of intelligence as a single, measurable human capability. Although his work has not had the same impact on schooling as Gardner's theory of multiple intelligences, Sternberg's idea of three key components of intelligence offers some interesting ways of thinking about learning. The components are:

- *analytical intelligence*: the ability to complete academic tasks that are well defined and typically have a single correct answer;
- *creative or synthetic intelligence*: the ability to use existing knowledge and skills and to see things from alternative perspectives; and
- *practical intelligence*: the ability to understand what needs to be done in a specific setting and then to be able to do it.

Running across all of the debates about cognitive development is the concern of researchers to explain how people learn. Yet, as the brief overview above illustrates, the field is ever contested as different aspects of learning are able to be explained in different ways. Another interesting insight into views of learning is offered by Benjamin Bloom, who was involved in researching the assessment of learning.

Taxonomy of educational objectives

Benjamin Bloom was a cognitive psychologist who was interested in thinking and how it developed. His work was based on the measurement of educational objectives and he described tasks as being generally derived from one of three psychological domains: *cognitive* (ability to process and use information); *affective* (attitudes and feelings associated with learning); or *psychomotor* (manipulative and physical skills).

Bloom (1956) developed a taxonomy of educational objectives in the cognitive domain that offered a structure for categorising instructional objectives and assessment. His classification was based on the view that different learning objectives are based on different skills and abilities and therefore some objectives are easier (or harder) to attain than others and that difference should be reflected in the forms and status of assessment. For example, testing the memorisation of facts is easier than assessing higher-order thinking skills—a matter of memory versus understanding.

Bloom's taxonomy of educational objectives in the cognitive domain comprised six levels, each of which he considered was built up from the previous level. His six levels were:

- *knowledge*: remembering information; rote learning, memorising;
- *comprehension*: grasping the meaning of information; the ability to explain, interpret or restate ideas;
- *application*: using information, ideas and skills in different situations; problem solving;
- *analysis*: breaking information down into its constituent parts; looking for relationships between parts of information;
- *synthesis*: repackaging ideas and information into new forms; creativity and innovation; and
- *evaluation*: making judgements about the worth of material against criteria; reviewing and judging evidence.

Bloom's taxonomy of educational objectives in the affective domain comprised five levels:

- *receive*: open to ideas; willingness to listen;
- *respond*: actively participate in discussion; willingness to react;

- *value*: decide worth and relevance of ideas; prepared to commit to action;
- *organise*: qualify and quantify personal beliefs; offer reasons for personal position; and
- *characterise*: consistent behaviour in relation to values; internalise a personal philosophy.

Bloom's work had a major impact in education as it introduced the notion of higher-order thinking skills and drew serious attention to the difference in skills and abilities associated with different types of learning tasks.

Memory

In some ways, Bloom's work acts as a subtle reminder of the distinction Gilbert Ryle (1949) made between *knowing that* and *knowing how*. Knowing that equates to acquiring and remembering things as individual pieces of information; for example, knowing facts. Knowing how can be described as the ability to use information in practical situations—to put that knowledge to work. Bloom's taxonomy makes clear that moving beyond acquiring information, and being able to manipulate and use it as a progressive step in learning, is a more demanding cognitive function. Therefore, how knowledge might come to be more deeply embedded in a learner's memory so that it can be used in different ways in different contexts becomes an important issue.

It has been well demonstrated that our short-term memory has a relatively limited capacity and, as the term suggests, retains items for only a short period of time. Short-term memory has been shown to be able to hold seven, plus or minus two, elements at any given time. Therefore, if a learner is to retain knowledge for an extended period of time, that knowledge needs to be planted more deeply in a learner's memory. This occurs through the shift from short-term to long-term memory. It is in long-term memory that deeper processing of the original information can occur so that knowledge can be linked, developed and manipulated in a variety of ways and through a variety of experiences to build deeper understandings of the original ideas and information. Bloom's higher-order thinking is one way of

understanding how knowledge might become more deeply embedded in long term memory and mentally worked on to be useable and
applicable in different ways and in different situations.

Capturing and storing information is aided by a number of other
important mental processes. One of these is *selection*—the ability to
select the appropriate information among the competing stimuli
present in the environment. In teaching we do many things that are
designed to help our students select the information that we see as
important to their learning a particular concept. This is done through
activities such as creating cues (highlighting, bolding, underlining),
summarising the main points and drawing attention to the elements
that we think need to be selected to form a base from which students'
learning might progress.

Chunking is another useful mental process and can be very
helpful in not only changing what can be stored in short-term
memory but also the manner in which it may be structured and
restructured in long-term memory. For example, the 'seven plus
or minus two' rule for short-term memory can easily be challenged by the way in which the individual elements are viewed.
Trying to remember a series of individual numbers is limited
by this rule. However, if those numbers are chunked in a different form (for example, as room numbers, telephone numbers,
or some other *aide de memoir*) the capacity to hold those numbers in short-term memory dramatically changes. Similarly,
moving from individual elements to larger chunks of combined
information can make an enormous difference not only to how
that information is stored in long-term memory, but also what it
might be linked to, and therefore how it can enhance, a learner's
understanding of that information through deeper processing in
the long-term memory. Again, how we help our students think
about how to chunk information has important implications for
learning.

Processing is also important, and refers to the ways in which information is manipulated and worked through so that it is understood at
more than a superficial level in order to carry more meaning for the
learner. When we ask students to compare and contrast, or to analyse
and describe, we are creating tasks that are designed to encourage

processing of information in ways that fundamentally change how that information is structured and connected in their thinking.

All of these cognitive strategies help to embed ideas and information in a student's memory and therefore develop their learning.

Deep and surface learning

The nature of processing obviously influences how learners make sense of information. Processing can be an active process in which the learner purposefully attempts to integrate new information with their existing ideas and knowledge (*deep processing*) or it may involve simply trying to remember facts in unconnected ways (*surface processing*). Ference Marton and Roger Saljo (1976) researched this facet of learning by asking students to read a piece of text. They then interviewed the students about the way they had processed the information. As a consequence they found that the students could be categorised into one of two groups. The approach of one group of students revolved around working hard to memorise what they thought might be the important bits of information in the passages (which they described as a surface approach). In contrast the other group worked hard to determine the author's basic argument; that is, this group of students tried to develop an understanding of the text (which they described as a deep approach). Hence, that which has come to be known in the literature as the surface approach to learning is linked to the intention to memorise or rote learn while a deep approach is commonly linked to the intention of developing understanding and creating meaning for the individual learner.

Even though a surface approach can be interpreted as being a superficial way of learning and the deep approach as a more active and critical approach, such a distinction should not necessarily be viewed as the only conclusion. For example, an active learner may choose to adopt a surface approach by scanning large amounts of information in order to develop a manageable big-picture view of a situation rather than become bogged down in trying to make sense of things that may not warrant the expenditure of time and energy necessary to do so. Therefore, although deep and surface can be helpful descriptors for differentiating between approaches to learning, it does not necessarily follow that deep learning is good and surface learning is bad. One reason for resisting the good/bad conclusion is linked to another important cognitive function that serves a major role in learning—*metacognition*.

Metacognition is the ability to monitor and control one's own processes of thinking and is perhaps best recognised by the types of questions learners ask themselves when trying to construct meaning from information. We are all familiar with the flood of questions that pop into our head when confronted by challenging information, ideas or tasks: 'What does this mean?', 'What do I know about this topic?', 'How does this information link to what I already know?' and, at the end of the task, questions such as, 'How well did I complete the task?', 'What else should I have done?', 'What could I have done differently?', 'Am I satisfied with my efforts?' These questions are all examples of metacognition—questioning our own thinking—which is very important in extending our learning. Hence, as noted above, choosing to use a surface approach to learning may well be a metacognitive response to the demands of learning in that context. When considered from this perspective, the purpose for learning looms large as a significant driver for the quality of learning because a learner's awareness of purpose drives quality of learning. If a surface approach becomes a subconscious default approach, deep processing will be less likely to occur. Conversely, if all learning involves a deep approach, the time, energy and effort required may make it very difficult for that learner to differentiate between tasks and make reasonable choices about what to learn and how. Being conscious of one's own thinking (and questioning that thinking) therefore matters in monitoring one's own learning.

Marton and Saljo's research has had an enduring effect on views of learning and has been taken up in many fields of study as a way of helping students to make informed choices about how they approach their learning. For example, the Higher Education Academy Engineering Subject Centre (HEA, 2008) offers an overview for putting theory into practice in regard to deep and surface learning and how teachers' and students' approaches influence the nature of learning (see Table 2.1).

Table 2.1 Deep and surface learning

	Deep learning	Surface learning
Definition	Examining new facts and ideas critically, and tying them into existing cognitive structures and making numerous links between ideas.	Accepting new facts and ideas uncritically and attempting to store them as isolated, unconnected items.
Characteristics	Looking for meaning. Focusing on the central argument or **concepts** needed to solve a problem. Interacting actively. Distinguishing between argument and evidence. Making connections between different modules. Relating new and previous knowledge. Linking course content to real life.	Relying on rote learning. Focusing on outward signs and the **formulae** needed to solve a problem. Receiving information passively. Failing to distinguish principles from examples. Treating parts of modules and programs as separate. Not recognising new material as building on previous work. Seeing course content simply as material to be learnt for the exam.
Encouraged by students	Having an intrinsic curiosity in the subject. Being determined to do well and mentally engaging when doing academic work. Having the appropriate background knowledge for a sound foundation. Having time to pursue interests, through good time management. Positive experience of education leading to confidence in ability to understand and succeed.	Studying a degree for the qualification and not being interested in the subject. Not focusing on academic areas, but emphasising others (e.g. social, sport). Lacking background knowledge and understanding necessary to understand material. Not enough time/too high a workload. Cynical view of education, believing that factual recall is what is required. High anxiety.

	Deep learning	Surface learning
Encouraged by teachers	Showing personal interest in the subject. Bringing out the structure of the subject. Concentrating on and ensuring plenty of time for key concepts. Confronting students' misconceptions. Engaging students in active learning. Using assessments that require thought, and requires ideas to be used together. Relating new material to what students already know and understand. Allowing students to make mistakes without penalty and rewarding effort. Being consistent and fair in assessing declared intended learning outcomes, and hence establishing trust.	Conveying disinterest or even a negative attitude to the material. Presenting material so that it can be perceived as a series of unrelated facts and ideas. Allowing students to be passive. Assessing for independent facts (short answer questions). Rushing to cover too much material. Emphasising coverage at the expense of depth. Creating undue anxiety or low expectations of success by discouraging statements or excessive workload. Having a short assessment cycle.

Source: compiled from Biggs (1999), Entwistle (1988) and Ramsden (1992) in Houghton, 2004

An interesting aspect of Table 2.1 is how the use of deep and surface learning as a dichotomy can also create difficulties and contradictions in ways similar to that of the theory–practice gap. So it is important to always be conscious of purpose as a driver for the nature of learning.

Elements of memory

Another way of thinking about learning is to consider some of the elements that influence how information is gathered and used and therefore shape the nature of learning itself. Richard White, in his book *Learning Science* (1988), which was informed by the work of psychologists such as Gagné, Ausubel, Piaget, Wittrock and Marton, described seven elements of memory that he considered important in helping to describe the sorts of things people know. His seven elements included: strings, propositions, images, episodes, intellectual skills, motor skills and cognitive strategies.

Strings are 'a sequence of words or symbols recalled as a whole in an invariate form' (White, 1988: 23). Strings are most commonly recognised in the ability to remember such things as poetry, songs, telephone numbers or sayings. An interesting aspect of strings is that they are learnt by repetition so that they might be recalled quickly and easily and in the correct form. Therefore, remembering the trigger term or phrase leads to recalling the whole. For example, 'Too many cooks, spoil the broth', or 'Thirty days hath September, April, June and November . . .' show how one part of the string evokes the whole.

Propositions 'make up a large proportion of people's memories. In colloquial terms, propositions are the things people "know" . . . They are known as "facts" . . . "beliefs" or "opinions" . . . As far as memory is concerned there is no difference between facts and opinions. Both are beliefs which are stored similarly, and may be learned simply' (White, 1988: 27).

Images are mental pictures. However, it is important to recognise that images are not solely visual because they can relate to any of the five senses. Images are often stored as archetypes (for example, a flower, tree, or scientist) and many of these are taught to us. Of course we can also develop images ourselves, as often happens when imagining a particular situation—the description causes us to create an image or snapshot of that situation in our mind.

Episodes are 'records of experience, memories of the events, occurrences we took part in or witnessed . . . Our whole notion of self is bound up with the recollections of things we have done and experienced' (White, 1988: 31). Episodes are important in learning because they dramatically influence students' perceptions of context and the way they function within, or feel about, that context.

Intellectual skills can be categorised into divisions: discriminations, classes and rules. Discrimination is the ability to determine those things that are the same and those things that are different.

'Discriminations can be a source of unexpected trouble in teaching. Once you have acquired a discrimination skill, it is difficult to comprehend that another person cannot see the difference that is obvious to you'. (White, 1988: 35) Classing is a skill that is frequently used and in many cases happens almost instantaneously. It involves making judgements about features that things have in common (or not) in order to classify them in particular ways to allow us to group and name. Rules include procedures and algorithms and are highly specific. 'Rules must be defined so that, barring lucky guesses and slips through inattention, each individual consistently will be able, or unable, to perform any exercise which fits the definition.' (White, 1988: 38) Common algorithms are used in calculating mathematical formulae, constructing graphs, or allocating notes appropriately to bars according to the key signature in music.

Motor skills 'are memories of how to make muscle movements of a complex form. They share the attributes of intellectual skills of being analysable into prerequisite movements and, once learned, of being applicable to a class of tasks' (White, 1988: 40).

Cognitive strategies 'are very general skills, each frequently activated in diverse acts of learning and doing. Examples are determining goals, working out options, judging likelihood of success, reflecting on the meaning of new knowledge, searching out associations between elements of knowledge, generalizing and deducing' (White, 1988: 40). Cognitive strategies then are the ways in which learners question their learning.

In describing these seven elements of memory White makes an argument about the development of understanding, linking it to ways in which learning (or lack thereof) can aid or inhibit that process. His point is that each of the elements of memory serves to develop knowledge in different ways and through different processes. In so doing, understanding is developed as new knowledge and skills are more deeply processed and linked so that they can be used to manipulate the information in ways that benefit the learner and therefore further develop understanding.

In White's view, teaching needs to be responsive to the different elements of memory in appropriate ways in order to enhance students' understanding of the content being studied. He suggests that in many instances, both teachers and students have 'scripts' that influence how they approach their work, which results in stereotypical views of what teaching looks like and what school learning generally involves. By developing a deeper understanding of learning, the traditional scripts of school teaching and learning can be challenged in productive ways so that practice is more informed and more responsive to learners' needs.

As this brief overview illustrates, there are many different ways of looking into the nature of learning. So in closing the chapter, it is perhaps helpful to briefly consider one of the big-picture views of learning from a cognitive perspective that has attracted attention and has had some impact on schooling: the theory of *constructivism*.

Constructivism

In many ways, the work of Piaget and Vygotsky can be seen as forerunners to the development of what has come to be known as constructivism. To many educators, constructivism offers a common-sense explanation for how students learn. Constructivism suggests that learners construct knowledge by developing mental schemas that allow them to progressively add new information to existing knowledge with the result being the development of increasingly complex cognitive structures—the development of personal understanding. This occurs as students interact with their environment through social and collaborative processes.

As is the case with many big-picture theories, variations are introduced to describe or limit how the theory might be used to explain different situations: for example, psychological constructivism (Piagetian-based view with a focus on the individual); social constructivism (Vygotskian-based view with a focus on social interaction); and radical constructivism (Ernst von Glasersfeld's (1995) view that there is no alternative to learning but to construct knowledge based on one's own experiences).

Constructivism is a theory of learning that has in some cases been confused with descriptions of teaching. In essence, the link between constructivism and teaching is in how a teaching environment might be organised to support learning in a constructivist manner. Therefore, the underlying principles of constructivism can be helpful in thinking about how to structure teaching, but constructivism itself is a theory of learning. Some of the important learning principles of constructivism include: learning by doing; regulating one's own learning; building individual meaning in a situation or experience; and learning with and from others.

Overview

This chapter has been designed to briefly consider some of the aspects of learning that help to shape the manner in which a learner's understanding can be developed. In considering the range of views associated with thinking about learning it also helps to illustrate why teaching is so complex and how important it is to pay careful attention to the relationship between teaching and learning. It is this relationship that is at the heart of pedagogy and that is what is examined in the following chapter.

3
Pedagogy

The term 'pedagogy' is commonly used in one of two ways. In countries such as the United Kingdom, the United States, Canada, Australia and New Zealand, pedagogy is often used as a synonym for teaching. However, as has been noted a number of times in the literature, when described in terms of its European traditions pedagogy entails more than just teaching. Van Manen (1999) described pedagogy as the art and science of educating children—based on its Greek roots (to lead a child). When viewed from this perspective, pedagogy is concerned with the relationship between learning and teaching. Understanding this interplay between teaching and learning *and* learning and teaching is an important shift in focus from teaching alone because it really means that the two exist together. The fact that teaching influences learning and learning influences teaching, and the way that is done, offers insights into the science of educating.

If we think about pedagogy in terms of its European roots, then teaching and learning become more purposely linked such that stereotypical views (and practices) of teaching as telling must be challenged because any sense of pedagogy as a one-way process is counter to its underlying meaning. In one sense, Paulo Freire (1972) highlighted this point through his description of the banking method of teaching (information being deposited) which, as he made clear, is far from education as transformation.

Therefore, thinking about pedagogy as the relationship between teaching and learning is important because it fundamentally changes what we look at and why when considering notions of quality in practice. There is clearly a major difference between a classroom in which the transmission of information dominates and one in which students' experiences shape the nature of teaching and learning. In a teaching and learning environment, where experiences matter, pedagogy is able to be recognised through such things as intellectual challenge, support for learning, linking and relevance, and sensitivity to diversity, all of which extend learning beyond the subject matter alone. That means that the way we teach should be a consequence of reflection on the learning possibilities and/or limitations of a particular episode. If that is the case, then the teaching approach we develop is a result of our pedagogical reasoning; that is, a teaching procedure used for a particular reason to achieve a particular purpose in response to the nature of the teaching and learning environment. Approaching teaching in that way is dramatically different from simply trying to implement a fun activity in the classroom in order to ameliorate students' lack of interest in the content of the subject.

Pedagogy involves two aspects of learning. The first is associated with what and how students are learning; the second is about the teacher as a learner—learning about teaching and building expertise. Thinking about pedagogy in this way helps to highlight teaching as an educative process for both partners in the relationship rather than a set of technical skills. Researchers have illustrated how learning through reflection on experience is important in the development of such expertise and expert–novice studies have consistently demonstrated that:

- novices tend to view experiences and events as separate and isolated whereas experts search for patterns and relationships;
- novices' approaches to planning arc not as organised and focused as those of experts, who carefully plan to meet their goals; and
- novices tend to be captured by the immediacy of the situation whereas experts are not only aware of their thoughts and actions (in action), but also the impact of these on their practice.

Therefore, the development of pedagogical expertise can be viewed as a learning process that combines theory and practice in ways that help to build knowledge. Teaching is not just a matter of doing, it is about the doing informing the practice and how that doing is captured, reflected on, deconstructed and reconstructed in a genuine effort to learn from experience. (The obvious similarities between this and expectations for students' learning further demonstrates the reciprocal nature of teaching and learning and why understanding pedagogy in this way matters.)

Learning through experience is crucial because although we may understand content particularly well, the development of pedagogical expertise involves knowledge of much more than just the subject matter. For example, there may be a number of different ways of introducing a topic and so, through experimenting with and reflecting on such experiences, we learn how to develop an ever-expanding repertoire of general teaching procedures. In addition to this, there may be particular elements of the content that, over time, we learn to teach in particular ways because it helps our students make sense of it.

Pedagogical expertise, then, comes to the fore when this knowledge is sorted, filtered and analysed in concert with views of student learning, such that the pedagogical experiences we create are responsive to the learning demands inherent in the situation. Hence, teaching is a process embedded in relationships—relationships between: thinking and doing; theory and practice; students and teachers; students and content; students and students, and so on. In all cases, finding an appropriate balance is important for creating meaningful pedagogical experiences because as Freire reminds us:

> We must not negate practice for the sake of theory. To do so would reduce theory to a pure verbalism or intellectualism. By the same token, to negate theory for the sake of practice . . . is to run the risk of losing oneself in the disconnectedness of practice. It is for this reason that I never advocate a theoretic elitism or a practice ungrounded in theory, but the unity between theory and practice. In order to achieve this unity, one must have an epistemological curiosity. (Freire & Macedo, 1995: 382)

It is not hard to see then why learning about teaching is difficult, and sometimes confusing and frustrating. The problematic nature of practice in itself creates uncertainty and, yet, to learn more about practice requires us to choose to increase that level of uncertainty through risk taking in order to experiment with our practice. Learning to be comfortable with uncertainty is then part of what it means to become a learner of teaching and is at the heart of that which supports the development of pedagogical expertise, as the following anecdote illustrates.

Winning them over

Enveloped in an impending shadow of doom I realised I had 7D next lesson. 'I'm sure they're not really human,' I thought to myself as I reflected on our previous music class in which Beethoven's *Fifth Symphony* was reduced to farce. It was all too fresh in my mind.

I could feel the pounding in my chest, which spread through my body like a fever, engulfing me head to toe as I tried desperately to control my breathing. 'Everything's okay, you'll be right, everything's okay,' I kept repeating to myself as I walked down the corridor to face them.

'It'll be okay,' I reminded myself again as I unlocked the classroom door. 'I've put in the work. I'll win them over today.'

The class straggled in, full of energy and attitude to burn.

'Good morning 7D.' I started desperately trying to speak over their noise.

'I'll call the roll. Maybe that will settle them down,' I thought to myself.

As I moved down the list of names I thought it would be a miracle if I got through this class alive. They were still very chatty so rather than trying to explain the lesson I just launched straight into it playing Jagged Edge's 'Let's Get Married'.

The song went for nearly four minutes and something amazing happened. There was complete silence. Twenty-six pairs of eyes peered at me. There were looks of confusion, or perhaps shock, awaiting some sort of explanation, seeking direction.

'Following up on your responses about the music you enjoy listening to,' I started, 'I thought it a good idea to look at some of these songs.'

> Silence remained but their facial expressions turned from puzzlement to interest. Was I dreaming? Did I have their full attention?
>
> 'OK, what's the driving force of the song we've just heard?' I asked.
>
> 'Rhythm!' Johnny called out enthusiastically from the back of the room.
>
> 'Yes, yes!' I was filled with a welcome feeling of triumph as students started critiquing the music with intelligent answers as they freely offered their opinions.
>
> Their excitement and interest built a foundation for a fantastic class discussion on the elements of music. The key was that what they were learning had some worth because they could relate to it. The same ideas I had for understanding Beethoven's Fifth were being played out through their music. I couldn't believe it—it actually worked. I finally had them.
>
> Through the discussion I finally understood what a sense of mutual respect and trust really felt like. They were my class at last!
> (Loughran, 2006: 141–2)

As the anecdote above suggests, new knowledge about practice emerges through the learning associated with taking risks in teaching and learning. However, taking risks is not meant to imply a haphazard or thoughtless approach. Rather, it is about the importance of experimenting with practice in ways that can inform and develop pedagogical expertise. Risk taking is about finding the balance in pedagogical relationships within the particular context at a particular time. Although that balance may vary with changes in context, learning from those experiences helps us to build a base from which future thinking about teaching *and* learning can be informed.

Knowledge of practice and why it matters

In their work 'Teachers' knowledge and how it develops', Munby et al. (2001) describe how, for a considerable period of time, there has been tension around conceptions of teachers' knowledge because of the differing, and in some cases conflicting, views about what that knowledge is and what counts as knowledge. The differences are often caught up in the philosophical definition of knowledge and whether or not that meaning should be applied to thinking about that which we as teachers know and are able to do.

As was noted in Chapter 1, when thinking about teaching the much maligned theory–practice gap attracts a great deal of attention. Not surprisingly, in the busyness of teaching, doing teaching requires a great deal of time and energy. Therefore, anything that draws us away from that task is often seen as an unnecessary distraction. Much of the help we look for in order to improve our practice is associated with finding new ideas and activities that will work in our classrooms.

Traditionally, academic knowledge of teaching has had little impact on practice and there are many reasons for this, including academic papers often using jargon and writing styles that are unfamiliar to teachers; academic knowledge of teaching usually not offering classroom activities; academics' questions of teaching being different to those that teachers ask about teaching; learning and classrooms that result in the academics' inquiries not always being particularly compelling to teachers, and so on. As a consequence we can sometimes view academic knowledge of teaching as so separate and distinct from our world of practice that it is difficult to see its value. On the other hand, academic researchers can also make the mistake of assuming that teachers are so consumed by practice that their work is atheoretical. Clearly, the reality is somewhere in between—just as Freire described earlier—and respect for both perspectives is crucial in ensuring an appropriate balance between theory and practice.

One way of understanding arguments about knowledge is by recognising and valuing the difference between what could be described as *public/codified knowledge* and *teachers' professional knowledge* of practice. Chapter 2 offered a range of views of knowledge about learning that could be described as public/codified knowledge (including the theories of Piaget, Bloom and others). That type of knowledge is what Gary Fenstermacher (1994) described as formal knowledge and it serves as a form that can be generalised and applied across contexts. On the other hand, that which he described as practical knowledge captures some of the elements of our ways of knowing because it is derived from our experiences of classroom teaching; it is different to formal knowledge, not better, not worse, just different; it serves a different purpose.

Public/codified knowledge is often allocated a status that is distinct from teachers' professional knowledge of practice because the common stereotype of the former is that the research is empirically based, scientifically conducted and rigorously reviewed. Of course the reality is that this is just one way in which research is conducted and reported—there are also many other genres derived from a range of methods, not all of which fit the stereotype. However, teachers' professional knowledge of practice further differs from public/codified knowledge in that it is often derived from teachers' personal experiences and is often described as a form of personal understanding. It is not necessarily generalisable (nor meant to be), and sadly, even within the profession, professional knowledge tends to be undervalued and seen as having a lower status than public/codified research knowledge.

It is interesting to ponder why it is that the type of knowledge that makes a difference for practice, and is so dependent on teachers' experience, abilities and skills, does not seem to be viewed as specialist knowledge in the way that practitioner knowledge is understood and valued in some other professions. Although teachers' professional knowledge of practice is different to the more traditional public/codified knowledge produced by educational researchers, both forms generally share a common concern; that the knowledge being developed should help to make a difference to students' learning.

Early last century, John Dewey (1929) stated that educational practices themselves must be the source of the ultimate problems to be investigated if we were to build a science of education. Knowledge of practice is crucial if education is to be advanced in ways that might be transformative, and such advancement lies in better understanding the problems derived from teaching and learning. Hence, there is an ongoing need to maintain a clear and sustained focus on pedagogy. Knowledge of teaching and learning should be such that it informs the practice setting. Therefore, addressing the theory–practice gap is essential in progressing teaching and learning in productive ways.

One of the barriers to better bridging the theory–practice gap is in the nature of some of the theory, pushed onto us by education bureaucracies, that does not necessarily lead to meaningful changes in practice. Rather, it tends to increase the amount of work that we, as teachers, have to manage and serves to draw us away from a concentration on our real classroom concerns. As a consequence, we often feel as though we are facing ongoing periods of constant change; no sooner is one set of education reforms introduced and implemented than a new innovation or reform takes its place.

Unfortunately, change of this kind often negatively influences our attitudes towards, and views about, theory. Yet when we happen upon theory that can assist teaching and learning, we quickly and enthusiastically convert that theory into practice. For example, Bloom's taxonomy (see pp. 25–6) is used by many teachers in very interesting ways to shape the nature of teaching and learning activities. By recognising how Bloom's different levels can shape students' learning, teachers have created thoughtful pedagogic experiences that draw on the different types of thinking associated with Bloom's taxonomic levels (see Chapter 9: Metacognition). In a similar way, teachers have also incorporated approaches to classroom practice based on DeBono's (1992) thinking hats (see Chapter 6: Linking), and Gardner's (1983) theory of multiple intelligences (see pp. 23–4).

By using these theoretical frameworks, teachers consistently demonstrate an important aspect of their specialised knowledge of practice. They recognise how a particular theory of teaching or learning can help to explain episodes, experiences and events that they have observed in their own classrooms; the theoretical explanation is something with which they readily identify. They then translate that public/codified knowledge into a useable form through a teaching activity that is appropriate to their classroom context.

It needs to be understood that the skills associated with managing this translation of theory into practice is a specialised form of knowledge that is deeply embedded in our experiences of risk taking and experimenting with practice. Through that process, we become expert at abstracting the specific from the generalisable in ways that allow us to apply that knowledge in meaningful ways in our particular context.

One way of understanding why this aspect of teachers' knowledge of practice is not so highly regarded within the profession is because we do not tend to talk about our teaching from a theoretical perspective. Instead, we commonly talk about and share the activities that we have created because it is in those elements of our knowledge that we have something tangible, immediately applicable and useable in the classroom. Again, it is not that our knowledge is better or worse than public/codified knowledge, it is just different. Part of the reason for the difference can also be explained by the need for relevance; relevance in relation to purpose. Purpose in this case is about the need for knowledge to have meaning in our practice in ways that we can see will influence our students' learning. If it fails the currency for practice test, then it becomes more of a distraction and so tends to be relegated accordingly.

Marilyn Cochran-Smith and Susan Lytle (1999) touched on this notion of purpose in a different way when they described teachers' professional knowledge in terms of: knowledge *for* practice; knowledge *in* practice; and knowledge *of* practice. Through each of these three forms of teachers' knowledge, Cochran-Smith and Lytle built an argument for conceptualising teaching as based on inquiry (an issue taken up in more detail in Part 3: Professional Learning). They described it as being:

> intended to offer a closer understanding of the knowledge generated in inquiry communities, how inquiry relates to practice and what teachers learn from inquiry ... the term inquiry as stance describe[s] the positions teachers ... take toward knowledge and its relationships to practice ... it involves making problematic the current arrangements of schooling; the ways knowledge is constructed, evaluated and used; and teachers' individual and collective roles in bringing about change. (1999: 288–9)

If teaching is understood as a form of inquiry, then it stands to reason that pedagogic relationships need to be opened up for serious examination. In so doing it may well be that a greater appreciation of what we know, need to know and are able to do is recognised and articulated. As teachers we actively develop, assess and adjust our professional knowledge in light of our own experiences of teaching. What we are not so involved in is articulating that knowledge. Thus making our professional knowledge of practice explicit is crucial.

Peter Grimmett and Alan MacKinnon (1992) describe teachers' professional knowledge in terms of *craft knowledge*. Through the construct of craft knowledge they offer a way of thinking about practice as being based on principles that teachers might conceptualise and in so doing help to make the tacit more explicit: '[craft knowledge could then] act as a sensitising framework to teachers . . . [and] constitute a broadly conceived set of principles . . . [to] provoke discussion and intellectual ferment; they would stimulate teachers to reflect on why they enact certain classroom practices and resist others' (Grimmett & MacKinnon, 1992: 438).

A concrete example of thinking about knowledge of practice is through Lee Shulman's (1986) notion of *pedagogical content knowledge* (PCK). PCK is the knowledge of teaching particular subject matter in a particular way for a particular reason to enhance student learning. PCK, then, is a very specialised form of teachers' knowledge of practice whereby the relationship between practice and the subject matter being taught is the major focus.

In recent times, studies of science teaching and learning have focused on what PCK looks like and how it might be described for others. In an explication of PCK based on extensive studies of expert science teachers in action, two components have been described as working together to demonstrate the thinking that underpins science teachers' PCK (Loughran, Berry & Mulhall, 2006). One component has been described as *content representation* (CoRe; see Table 3.1). The other is designed around windows into practice (Pedagogical and Professional-experience Repertoires—PaP-eRs).

CoRe captures well a diverse range of knowledge that teachers have of particular content and how that knowledge is adjusted and adapted in, and for, practice. CoRe illustrates how subject matter is not viewed by expert science teachers as sequential blocks of information to be delivered to students. Rather, it is constructed in terms of the big ideas that direct the ways in which the content might be conceptualised so that it makes sense to learners in a much more holistic and connected fashion.

In considering the prompts in the left-hand column of Table 3.1, questions are asked of the content in terms of purpose in relation to practice. These prompts make clear how expert science teachers develop their thinking about their teaching in relation to the content such that what they do, how they do it, and why they do it is clear and explicit.

It is in the shift from knowledge of practice being tacit to explicit that challenges in teaching emerge and expertise comes to the fore. It is also where the balance between theory and practice is realised and could well be a path that leads to placing a higher value on teachers and teaching both within and outside of the profession.

Table 3.1 Content representation (CoRe)

	Big idea A	Big idea B	Big idea C	Big idea D
What you intend the students to learn about this idea				
Why it is important for students to know this				
What else you know about this idea (that you do not intend students to know yet)				
Difficulties or limitations connected with teaching this idea				
Knowledge about students' thinking that influences your teaching of this idea				

	Big idea A	Big idea B	Big idea C	Big idea D
Other factors that influence your teaching of this idea				
Teaching procedures (and particular reasons for using these to engage with this idea)				
Specific ways of ascertaining students' understanding or confusion around this idea (including likely range of responses)				

A language of teaching and learning

Being a teacher carries strong expectations about the act of teaching from oneself, students, school and the community, and these expectations may sometimes be in conflict. Not surprisingly, then, the need to accumulate a diverse range of ways to do teaching can easily dominate views of practice because of this spectrum of expectations. Developing a 'bag of teaching tricks' is important, but this is a very limited perspective on what it means to be a teaching professional. Purposely developing one's professional knowledge of teaching and being able to unpack that knowledge is another way of viewing the development of professional expertise.

The research literature demonstrates that for many teachers, knowledge of practice is not only tacit but is also difficult to talk about (Zanting, Verloop & Vermunt, 2003). However, talking about practice can dramatically change with the right sort of prompts. For example, Zanting et al. found that by talking about practice with teachers that focused on such things as classroom observation (paying careful attention to the *why* of practice), stimulated recall, concept maps, interviews, repertory grids or narratives, the nature of the discussion changed and the theoretical perspectives underpinning practice began to emerge.

In most professions there is a specialised language that is important for sharing the knowledge of practice. For those outside a particular field of work, that specialised language can, in some cases, be viewed as exclusionary jargon—others are unable to be fully involved in conversations about that knowledge and practice. Interestingly, because so much of the work of teaching seems familiar, the use of a specialised language of teaching and learning is sometimes derided—both within and outside of the profession—and further adds to perceptions of a theory–practice gap. However, a specialised language of teaching and learning is important because it allows sharing of understanding in ways that can be commonly used within the profession and shift the intention of sharing from an over-reliance on activities that work to more informed examination of the pedagogical intent underpinning practice. In essence, then, a language of teaching and learning is important because it allows us to discuss what we know and how we know it in meaningful ways which, inevitably, are embedded in understandings of practice at a much deeper level than the superficial understandings of those not so intimately involved in the work of teaching. Such a language then makes sharing professional knowledge both efficient and helpful for those of us who use that knowledge in our daily practice.

One example of a language of teaching and learning is in Jeff Northfield's *summary statements* (see Chapter 11, Loughran & Northfield, 1996). Northfield created summary statements as a way of reminding himself about that which he came to know about his teaching as a result of reflecting on his practice over the course of a full school year. In so doing, he developed a way of documenting and sharing his professional knowledge of teaching based on drawing generalised understandings of teaching and learning from an enormous array of specific pedagogical events. He grouped his summary statements into categories (the nature of learning, the creation of conditions for learning, student perspectives on learning, the process of teaching and learning), which allowed him to extract the essence of his learning about practice from his experiences with his students. For example, he noted that 'quality learning requires learner consent' (Loughran & Northfield, 1996: 124). This statement became a constant reminder to him that no matter how much he wanted his students to learn, in the end they were responsible for their own learning and that in many ways his job was to create ways of inviting his students to choose to learn through engaging with pedagogic situations. It is not hard to identify with Northfield's desire for students to learn and how that played out in the classroom activities he created and initiated on a regular basis. However, no matter how much we as teachers want students to learn, as Northfield demonstrated we cannot do the learning for them. Therefore, teaching looks very different when directed by a view that high quality learning requires learner consent, compared to teaching in which it is assumed that learning can be mandated.

Another summary statement that Northfield noted was 'teacher change precedes student change' (Loughran & Northfield, 1996: 124). This statement offers insights into the nature of change and hints at the expectations for behaviour necessary to accompany that change. If we expect students to accept responsibility for their own learning, then clearly our practice must be constructed in such a way as to allow that responsibility to be recognised and grasped by our students. At one level it is difficult to imagine how students might be active and responsible learners if the type of teaching they experience totally directs what they do, how and why. Therefore, in expecting students to be active learners, we need to reflect on how we construct pedagogic experiences that will encourage the desired behaviours in them. For those changes to occur in learning, changes in teaching may well be necessary, thus teacher change precedes student change.

Northfield's work, particularly his summary statements, illustrates the value in recognising and articulating knowledge of practice. As has been pointed out in the literature, expertise in ways of communicating and sharing professional knowledge is a hallmark of scholarship (Shulman, 1999). The next section examines such scholarship in detail.

Articulating a knowledge of practice

There have long been calls for the need to pay more attention to the processes of teaching and learning (Calderhead, 1988; Dewey, 1964). In so doing, there is also a need for a shared language of practice so that knowledge derived from such investigations might be understood and shared in helpful ways. Accounts from teacher research and other forms of practitioner inquiry offer insights into what such a language might look like and how it might be portrayed and shared with others. The work of Amanda Berry suggests one way of thinking about how to conceptualise professional knowledge of practice.

As a high school teacher, Berry spent some time in a shared teaching situation with a colleague, Philippa Milroy. Through that experience they were both confronted by the need to be able to explain to each other not just what they did in class, but also why, so that their pedagogic intent could be carried through in subsequent classes irrespective of which of them was doing the teaching. Therefore, although they planned the teaching together, depending on who taught the classes on a particular day there was a need for ongoing communication in ways that might ensure that their teaching and learning purposes were closely aligned and consistent.

Although they did not describe it at the time as an exploration of their professional knowledge of practice, their teacher research account of their experiences together, 'Changes that matter' (Berry & Milroy, 2002), can be seen as a way of beginning to explain what they came to know about student learning through a deeper examination of their shared teaching. They describe a number of critical incidents in their teaching that led them to extract meaning from the specific and apply it more generally across their teaching in ways similar to that of Jeff Northfield (above). For example, they describe the importance of:

- exposing assumptions;
- recognising and accepting responsibility;
- codified research knowledge (and the gaps therein);
- developing an atmosphere of trust;
- fruitfulness;
- learning to clearly speak;

- learning to really listen; and
- making the abstract concrete.

Each of the points above conveys something about the relationships inherent in teaching and learning that are so important in shaping what, as teachers, we know and are able to do. Jeff Northfield exposed an assumption in his statement that high quality learning requires learner consent. Berry and Milroy (2002) also recognised the importance of exposing assumptions and so became more adept at aligning their teaching with their expectations for their students' learning, as well as responding appropriately when that was not the case. By naming and framing, or creating labels to capture the essence of their learning from experience, they created a shared language to communicate their developing knowledge of practice with one another. Through that shared language they were able to express the pedagogic reasoning that underpinned their practice in such a way that they created their own jargon, as in the bullet points above. As a consequence, there was a shift in the way they talked about practice. Instead of searching for activities that worked, they focused on the learning outcomes they hoped to achieve through their teaching and then developed classroom activities to influence learning in the ways they intended. They were developing deeper understandings of pedagogy and expressing the subsequent learning about knowledge of practice through their own unique shared language.

When Amanda Berry made the transition from schoolteacher to teacher educator, the need to articulate her knowledge became all the more real. Although her articulation of her professional knowledge of practice was refined in a teacher education context, her *tensions* (see below) capture the essence of the problematic nature of teaching as an ongoing component of practice. When this is recognised and understood, it acts as a cornerstone to scholarship of teaching and focuses serious attention on what it means to be an expert pedagogue.

Tensions

Berry's articulation of tensions (2004, 2007) captures the ambiguities inherent in teaching. For Berry, tensions demonstrate how teaching is problematic in practice. As the intensive study of her teaching that led to the articulation of these tensions illustrates, teachers who are able to recognise and manage practice that is so heavily imbued in decision-making and uncertainty clearly possess specialised knowledge. The ability to articulate that knowledge is crucial in further developing and sharing wisdom of practice. Descriptions of her tensions follow.

Telling and growth

The tension between telling and growth is evident in the teacher's desire to provide information to students while at the same time seeking to create opportunities for them to build their own knowledge. This tension is also apparent in the teacher's attempts to acknowledge and respond to students' needs and concerns while still expecting to challenge them to move beyond those concerns.

Confidence and uncertainty

The tension between confidence and uncertainty is most apparent when attempting to manage the complexities and messiness of teaching while at the same time helping students to feel confident about how to proceed with their learning. There is also a certain sense of vulnerability from a teacher's perspective in being honest with students about the problematic nature of teaching while still maintaining students' confidence in the teacher as a leader.

Action and intent

The tension between action and intent comes to the fore when teachers feel conflicted by the desire to work towards a particular ideal but recognise the possibilty of jeopardising that ideal through the approach chosen to attain it. For example, when aiming to encourage students' independence as learners, a teacher might choose to step back from directing students' learning and, in so doing, some students might not respond appropriately because the teacher is no longer directing what they need to do.

Safety and challenge

The tension between safety and challenge is most palpable when teachers attempt to create a constructive learning experience that is also an uncomfortable one. For example, being confronted by a sense of cognitive dissonance, holding two contradictory ideas simultaneously, can lead learners to reconstruct their understanding of the situation and therefore develop a deeper understanding of it. However, it is also possible that the sense of discomfort experienced through the challenge can be too great and so the intended learning is not realised.

Acknowledging and building upon experience

The tension between acknowledging and building on experience is very challenging. It involves helping students to recognise what they know about their learning while encouraging them to see that there is more to learning than their existing school experience might suggest. For students (and teachers) to diverge from their existing schooling script is not easy. What students bring to their learning is important and needs to be acknowledged, yet at the same time learners need to be prepared to extend and develop that knowledge.

Planning and being responsive

The tension between planning for learning and being responsive to learning opportunities as they arise in practice requires a certain confidence and expertise that goes to the heart of managing the problematic nature of teaching. Being able to plan appropriate pedagogical experiences while at the same time being able to respond to the learning that emerges from those experiences requires skills and abilities honed through reflection on experience.

Being able to manage these tensions in our practice requires substantial expertise. There is a need to not only recognise how these tensions might impact our students' learning but to also be able to create and moderate them in the very act of teaching. In so doing, professional knowledge of practice is developed because:

> the tensions . . . do not exist in isolation from each other . . . [they] interact in practice . . . Instead of interpreting the tensions as situations that evoke despair and frustration, and trying to eliminate

them from one's work, [professionals] begin to reframe them as elements that are necessary and pleasurable for the growth and learning that they bring [of teachers' professional knowledge]. (Berry, 2004: 1325, 1327)

When we recognise and respond to the problematic nature of teaching through such things as tensions, we begin to expose our professional knowledge of teaching in ways that encourage us to question, critique and analyse practice in professionally rewarding ways. It is through these processes that such knowledge can come to be better understood, better valued and better used in shaping the nature of pedagogy and highlighting the scholarship in, and expertise of, teaching.

Overview

This chapter has attempted to create a new way of thinking about how to challenge the perceived theory–practice gap in teaching. A shared language of teaching and learning is the foundation for professional knowledge that is so important in being better informed about the nature of pedagogy and developing our pedagogical expertise. However, this chapter should not be interpreted as suggesting that there is one true and correct way of expressing teachers' professional knowledge. Rather, the intention is to highlight the fact that for knowledge to carry genuine meaning in practice, it needs to be able to be readily identified and useable in the practice setting; it needs to inform teaching.

Scholarship in teaching requires professional knowledge of practice to be publicly available for critical review and development. Putting such knowledge to use is a choice for each of us as individuals. However, choosing to do something about it is a professional expectation.

Part 2
Knowledge of Practice in Action

Part 2 of this book builds on Part 1 by illustrating how teachers' professional knowledge might be described and articulated through the development and use of a common language of practice.

Each of the chapters in Part 2 is based on a big-picture self-explanatory term derived from knowledge of teaching and learning. Working from the big picture, the processes of teaching and learning associated with the given term are fully detailed so that the underlying theoretical aspects are logically and clearly explained. The theory is then demonstrated in practice through concrete examples from a range of subject areas and year levels.

Importantly, although the concrete examples in each chapter are designed to show how teachers' professional knowledge is recognisable through practice, it is not intended that the teaching activities, procedures or strategies outlined become substitutes for that knowledge. Rather, they are a way of demonstrating how professional knowledge of practice is important in enhancing teaching and learning, a way of identifying quality teaching and learning within the profession. In so doing, the ways in which a language of teaching and learning can then help to define quality emerges as a strong component of professional practice. It is also shown that through the conscious use of such language, the development of pedagogical reasoning and expertise will assist teachers in moving beyond teaching activities alone. As a consequence, the ways in which teachers might then conceptualise and discuss what they do, and how and why, will become linked in holistic ways to the importance of knowledge of practice *for* practice and in so doing help to define and demonstrate the nature of scholarship in teaching.

Each of the teaching procedures in Part 2 illustrates how teachers' professional knowledge is brought to life in the classroom through thoughtful pedagogic practices. While these procedures appear under specific topic areas (for example, linking or metacognition), as they fit well within those frameworks, they can also be adapted for different purposes and aspects of teaching and learning. Used in this way, they offer a broad range of procedures that are applicable across all the teaching fields.

In the hands of a skilful teacher, teaching procedures move beyond simple technical applications or fun activities to offer insights into the specialist knowledge and skills of an expert pedagogue. However, as is the case with all good teaching, teaching procedures are able to be adapted, adjusted and altered to suit the particular context. When knowledge of subject matter and teaching are combined into practice to shape the nature of pedagogy, teachers' professional knowledge becomes tangible and significant. This is something that needs to be understood, more highly prized and specifically valued within the profession. The teaching procedures in Part 2 go some way to revealing what that might look like and how that may be done.

4
Prior knowledge

The ideas, information, beliefs and attitudes that learners bring with them to the classroom are some of the elements that comprise what could be termed as their *prior knowledge*, or knowledge gained prior to formal teaching. We are all familiar with the notion of prior knowledge and how it can influence our learning because, in one way or another, whether we are introduced to new things or are in a situation in which we are building on existing ideas, what we already know impacts on that learning.

Typically, when we are involved in, observe or hear about an experience or event, we link that event to the things that spring to mind that we already know, think or believe about that or a similar situation. In so doing, we bring to bear those ideas that we previously held in ways that we may or may not be conscious of, depending on how 'attached' we are to the existing ideas. For example, there are times when ideas that are firmly held prove difficult to shift or change. This is partly due to our prior knowledge having a bearing on how we view alternative perceptions of the same or a similar situation. In some cases, no matter how often we are told or how carefully something is explained to us, it is simply not sufficient to cause us to alter our existing worldview; we cling tightly to that which we already know, feel or believe.

Prior knowledge can take many forms. There are things that we learn, things that we are told, have heard about or seen, and situations that we have experienced. All of these shape our understanding. As a consequence, there is a continual building up of ideas that can be called upon in different ways.

Learning often involves some form of generalising insofar that the essence of the learning in one situation might be applied in another. Therefore, our prior knowledge may well comprise personal explanations of events that make sense to us, but although they might make sense, that does not necessarily mean they will be in accord with the explanations of others. This stands out most strikingly for science teachers when they explore students' explanations of many everyday phenomena. Although their explanations appear to make sense and fit their observations, they do not correspond with a scientist's explanation of the same event.

For example, winter is often seen as a time when people are most likely to catch a cold. It therefore seems quite natural to link the two and to think that catching a cold is caused by cold and wet weather, so staying warm and not getting caught in the rain might be ways of avoiding catching one. These ideas fit the way these events are typically understood, and are constructed to give a generalised picture of what it means to catch a cold. However, for the scientist, a cold is an infection caused by germs picked up from other people who sneeze, cough or in some other way transmit those germs to others. Research has shown that the most common way of catching a cold is from shaking hands with someone who has a cold—a person may have sneezed into their hands and then inadvertently passed the germ on to others through hand-to-hand contact.

A cold is a virus, and viruses have an incredible ability to keep changing. People do not tend to catch the same cold twice; that is, you may catch a cold but it isn't the same cold as last time. Because our immune system remembers the germs that it has fought in the past, the particular virus that caused a cold once is easily recognised by the immune system when it comes into contact with that virus again, thus that same virus isn't the cause of the next cold we catch. But, as the symptoms of a cold always seem to be the same, it is easy to assume that it is the same cold again.

In terms of prior knowledge (in this case erroneous prior knowledge), even the use of the term *a cold* is misleading, even more so when termed *the common cold*. Therefore, it is not difficult to see how a student's prior knowledge may get in the way when being taught the science of agents of disease. This is then a major problem for many science teachers and illustrates the importance of attempting to identify the range of students' prior knowledge in advance of teaching.

There is a vast literature on students' alternative conceptions (see, for example, Pfundt & Duit, 2000) and this work illustrates well how important it can be to not only be aware of, but be skilled at, working with students' prior knowledge if high quality learning is to be encouraged. But it is not just in science that prior knowledge can lead to difficulties with learning. The same applies across the curriculum from reading, through to history, mathematics and studies of culture. Prior knowledge involves learner feelings and attitudes, which can have a strong bearing on how students learn—or feel about learning—so prior knowledge is not only limited to information per se. This is well illustrated in Jeff Northfield's in-depth study of his high school teaching.

Jeff Northfield taught mathematics and science and was the home room teacher for a Year 7 class. He documented his attempts to foster active learning in his students in his book *Opening the classroom door* (Loughran & Northfield, 1996). In his study, it was most apparent to him that prior knowledge (particularly in the form of individual perceptions about subjects and ability) had a big influence on how some of his students approached their work.

The first meeting

In the first meeting with Jeff, Rhonda and Kathy felt it was important to identify themselves as failures in Maths when they introduced themselves.

Kathy: I'm Kathy and I am no good at Maths.
Rhonda: My name is Rhonda and I can't do Maths and I am not much better at other subjects.

The following excerpt from Northfield's journal illustrates how powerful students' views of themselves are and how that influences their expectations.

Journal: 16th June

Julie: What is my mark? . . . I know it will be awful.
Jeff: No, Julie, it was 44 out of 64 . . . that was quite good.
Julie: Oh . . . but the test was easy.
Jeff: Perhaps you are better than you think you are.
Julie: Mmm . . . I don't know . . . I don't think so.

. . . It is clear that some students accept they will not understand some areas of the work and so have no determination to fully understand everything (they give up easily). Why should they struggle and persist; not knowing some things is the normal state of affairs?' Julie, like some of her classmates in 7D, perceived school to be a place of inevitable failure. They had learned to be 'helpless'. (Loughran & Northfield, 1996: 64-5)

Building on students' prior knowledge

Unfortunately, as has been demonstrated time and again, many of the things that we experience as learners seem to be forgotten somehow when we assume the role of teacher.

Although it is obvious that prior knowledge is important in shaping the quality of learning, the 'teaching as telling' script is so strong that, as teachers, it is sometimes too easy to simply deliver information. We unconsciously assume that the ideas being delivered will be easily accommodated by the students as they tend to respond in ways designed to satisfy us that the ideas have been taken on board. However, in reality, the 'teaching as telling, learning as listening' game offers very little meaningful feedback as to how the new ideas have (or have not) been challenged or reconstructed as a consequence of being filtered by a learner's prior knowledge.

Clearly, then, prior knowledge is an important component of learning that we need to not only be aware of, but be prepared to work with in order to help develop our students' understanding. Students learn much more effectively when they are placed in positions where they are building on what they already know because they can link the new information to their existing information. In so doing, it is more likely that their curiosity will be aroused and that they will be encouraged to create and build their knowledge in ways that might help them to better understand the topic being studied.

When we work with students in ways that take into account their prior knowledge, new entry points to learning are made available to them that invite them to see a way in to the subject so that it makes sense to them. Research has illustrated that there is a strong relationship between prior knowledge and performance (Dochy, 1992; Dochy, Segers & Buehl, 1999). It also demonstrates that erroneous prior knowledge can hinder progress (Pintrich, Marx & Boyle, 1993) and so, one way or another, it is important that prior knowledge be addressed in and through our teaching.

There is little doubt that it is important to plan pedagogical experiences that build on students' prior knowledge. John Biggs (1999) suggests that deep learning results when the learning of new knowledge is connected to that which is already known. However, despite how simple it might sound to tap into students' prior knowledge in order to 'fix their understanding', there are many barriers that need to be broken down.

One of the recurring paradoxes of teaching is that despite our best efforts to find out what students think, they have actually learnt to be quite expert at playing 'guess what's in the teacher's head'. From a student's perspective, teachers' questions often appear to be designed to elicit a particular response. It is not surprising, then, that instead of finding out what they think, their answers are often an attempt to tell us what they think we want to hear (whether that is the intention of the questioning or not). Therefore, gaining genuine insights into students' prior knowledge requires pedagogical skills that need to be thoughtfully developed and refined.

At one level, a most important teaching behaviour that can help to decrease the effect of 'guess what's in the teacher's head' is the practice of *withholding judgement*. Withholding judgement means neither affirming nor negating students' responses. It requires the use of non-judgemental language and neutral non-verbal cues that encourage students to honestly offer their own ideas. For students to genuinely feel free to articulate and share their prior knowledge it is crucial that they do not feel as though their ideas are being judged. As language is so important in shaping the way that learners contribute to a conversation, withholding judgement is a teaching skill that encourages high quality interaction, particularly as discussion is such a dominant form of classroom activity.

As briefly touched on above, erroneous prior knowledge (misconceptions/alternative conceptions) is not corrected simply by telling students what's right and what's wrong in their memory banks. Helping students to see and hear the difference between what they know and what is being taught is important in helping them to address any sense of cognitive dissonance that may arise in a pedagogical situation.

Good teaching is about creating real opportunities for students to begin to determine for themselves how their knowledge needs to be structured and reconstructed in order to enhance the quality of their learning.

Teaching procedures: Prior knowledge

Probe of prior views

A probe of prior views offers students a range of ways of explaining an everyday event. Students choose the response they think best helps to explain the situation. In so doing, their responses help to illustrate their range of thinking about that particular event. The following probe of how electricity moves around a circuit to light a bulb is a good example of a *closed probe* of prior views. A closed probe offers specific alternatives—as in Figure 4.1—whereas an *open probe* provides a space for students to offer their own ideas.

A probe of prior views can be used as a pencil and paper diagnostic tool as in Figure 4.1, but could equally be used in a class discussion. In that way, students can attempt to convince others about their explanation of the phenomenon. By using this teaching procedure in this way students are encouraged to articulate their ideas publicly. By hearing their thinking out loud they are encouraged to address what they think and why as they come to recognise instances

Figure 4.1 Probe of prior views

A battery is connected to a torch bulb as shown. The bulb is glowing.

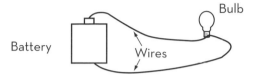

Which diagram below do you think best describes the electric current in the wires?

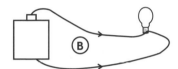

There will be *no* electric current in the wire attached to the base of the battery.

The electric current will be in the direction *towards* the bulb in *both* wires.

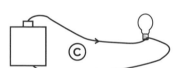

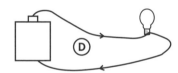

The direction of the electric current will be as shown. The current that will be *less* is the 'return' wire.

The direction of the electric current will be as shown. The current will be the *same* in both wires.

Source: Osborne & Freyburg, 1985: 25

of cognitive dissonance. (The affective component of learning is also important in terms of why a student might or might not be prepared to offer, defend or elaborate a view and can become very complex when teaching adolescent learners.)

Summary reflective writing/log book

Summary reflective writing is a procedure that can be used in many ways. It could be introduced in the final few minutes of a lesson when students are asked to reflect on what they have learnt and how it relates to what they already know. Figure 4.2 illustrates reflective writing following a lesson on Velcro. Students were asked how what they did in class that day connected to what they already knew about the topic.

Figure 4.2 Reflective writing: Velcro

> Today we studied Velcro. I wasn't very interested in Velcro but I was surprised to know it was invented in the 1940s. I had heard it was from the idea of hooks in a plant so it was good to know that was true. I'd also heard they use Velcro in the space shuttle but I'm not really sure that is true, how could it work in outer space and with such big and heavy things? How does someone think of an invention like Velcro? Why do you need a patent? Is that the same as copyright?

There are many ways of introducing reflective writing to students. The example in Figure 4.3 is based on the idea of students maintaining a reflective journal or log book (or 'thinking book'), which they use on a regular basis. Sue Swan conducted an extensive study with her class of eight-year-olds in which she examined how her use of thinking books influenced the way that her students thought about what they knew, what they wanted to know and what they learnt (Swan & White, 1994). The excerpt in Figure 4.3 illustrates how Swan was able to see how one student's (and some of her class mates') prior knowledge was likely to cause some confusion in relation to the topic of the First Fleet.

Figure 4.3 Reflective writing: The First Fleet

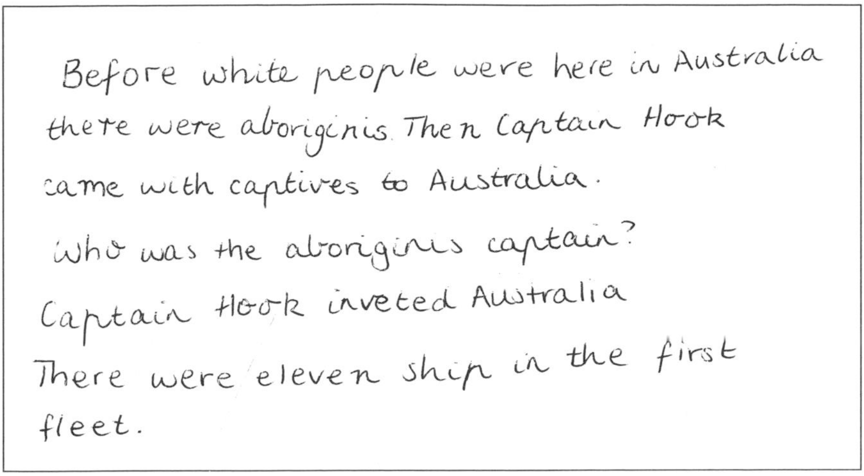

> Before white people were here in Australia
> there were aboriginis. Then Captain Hook
> came with captives to Australia.
> Who was the aboriginus captain?
> Captain Hook inveted Australia
> There were eleven ship in the first
> fleet.

Source: adapted from Swan & White, 1994: 51

Card sorting

Card sorting is designed as a way of beginning to investigate a particular topic, theme or unit of study. The major concepts that make up the theme are depicted on cards (making the card visually appealing is always helpful) and the students are asked to sort the cards into categories. Through that process, students' prior knowledge about the theme and the concepts underpinning the theme are revealed in ways that are informative to both students and teacher. For example, consider the card sort activity in Figure 4.4.

Another example of a card sort activity is one developed by English Heritage that deals with Victorian architecture, and uses two sets of cards. The first set contains some architectural intentions, for example, 'to impress people', or 'to demonstrate wealth'. The other set contains pictures of buildings. Students are divided into pairs and asked to choose one building, matching it with one or more of the intentions they think the building expresses, and explain their choices to the class (English Heritage, 2007).

Figure 4.4 Card sort exercise

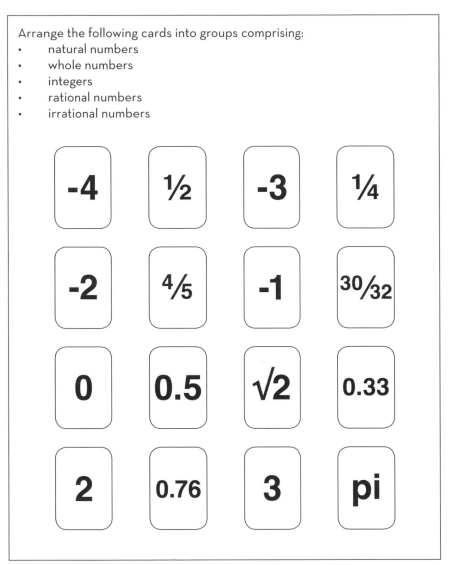

Arrange the following cards into groups comprising:
- natural numbers
- whole numbers
- integers
- rational numbers
- irrational numbers

Concept map

The term 'concept map' has been widely applied to a variety of ways of laying out concepts that are seen as integral to a theme or topic. Concept maps were developed by Joseph Novak at Cornell University (Novak & Godwin, 1984), the aim being to illustrate how someone sees the relations between items (concepts, ideas and objects) that comprise the main topic. An important aspect of a concept map is that it readily shows how the concepts are seen as fitting together because the exercise reveals how students perceive the relations between each. Concept maps can be very helpful at the start of a unit of work because they can help to demonstrate what a student brings to the topic.

For students who are unfamiliar with concept mapping it is important to let them practise making a concept map as it is a skill in its own right. Start with something that is not too complicated—approximately seven terms is a sufficient level of difficulty; too many terms can make the task far too demanding. It is also helpful if the concepts are able to be physically manipulated, by listing each on a separate card, because laying them out in a pattern in a way that satisfies the learner can take a number of iterations. There is no preordained pattern that needs to be adhered to although in some instances there may be a central concept to which the other concepts are tied. It may also be that some concept maps are hierarchical but, again, the point of this teaching procedure is to understand the students' perspective.

The following procedure is a good way to teach the skill of concept mapping. An example can be seen in Figure 4.5. Students are asked to:

1 Sort the concept cards and place to one side any that they do not know the meaning of or that seem unrelated to the other concepts.

2 Place the remaining cards on a sheet of paper and arrange them in any way that makes sense to them. Those terms that seem most closely related are probably best arranged nearest to one another. Those that seem least related are probably best arranged further apart. Make sure they leave enough space between cards to be able to write the relation between them easily.

3 Stick them to a sheet of paper when they have an arrangement that works, and have enough space between each to write.

4 Draw lines between the terms that they think are related (lines do not need to link every concept, only those that they think are related).

5 Write on each line what they think the relationship is between concepts. This is often easiest to do by asking them to think about the first concept as the first word in the sentence, and the second concept as the last word in the sentence. By putting an arrow head on the line they can indicate the direction in which the sentence is to be read.

6 Go back and check to see if any of the cards that they did not use now seem to have a place on their concept map. If so, remind them to draw their lines and write the nature of the links between the terms.

Figure 4.5 Concept map: Mount Vesuvius

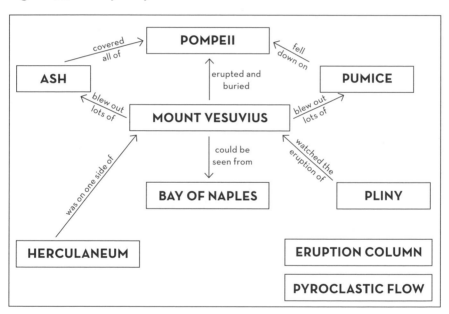

Concept maps have been used across all levels of schooling. The concept map in Figure 4.6 is from an early childhood setting in which the use of concept maps has been seen as:

effective in helping teachers identify students' prior knowledge and understandings and organise teaching and learning in a way that is meaningful to them. In fact, identifying students' pre-existing knowledge was the aim that led Novak and his team to the construction of the first concept map ... [and] once students learn how to externalise their understanding and create concept maps, their maps can be used as a way to monitor their conceptual development and assess their understanding and knowledge. (Birbili, 2006)

Figure 4.6 Concept map: Trees

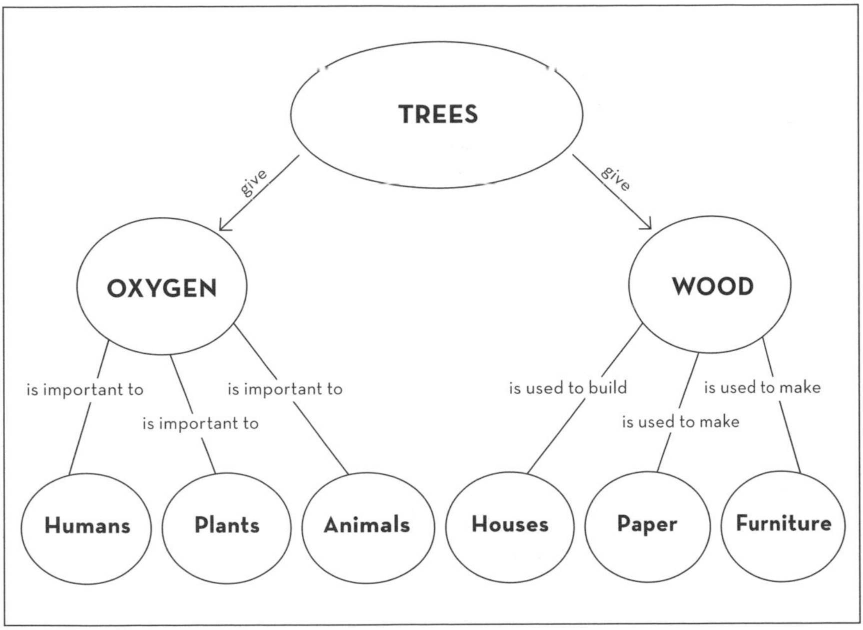

Source: Birbili, 2006

Another way of using a concept map to access students' prior knowledge is to ask them to choose a limited number of terms that they think are related to the topic to be studied and for them to then construct their concept map using those terms. The example in Figure 4.7 is illustrative of this approach.

Figure 4.7 Concept map: Spiders

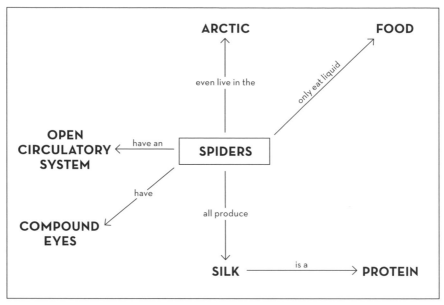

Know–What–Learn–How

The Know–What–Learn–How (KWLH) procedure helps students to explicitly draw on their prior knowledge. As either an individual or group activity, KWLH encourages active thinking. This procedure works well in advance of a lesson or new topic and can be progressively completed during the unit. It is also a good procedure for students to complete during the reading of text or other information. An example is shown in Table 4.1. The first two columns (Know and What) draw out students' prior knowledge, while the last two columns (Learn and How) offer ways of seeing how the prior knowledge has been used/addressed through the teaching/learning experience.

Table 4.1 Know-What-Learn-How (KWLH)

What we Know	**What** we want to find out	What we **Learn**ed	**How** we can learn more
Dinosaurs became extinct before people lived.	Why weren't people around when dinosaurs were around?	The deeper in the ground something is the longer ago it lived.	Research from the internet.
Not all dinosaurs are big.	How could such big things move quickly?		
Dinosaur fossils are found in special rocks.	Why are fossils only in some rocks?	Palaeontologists study fossils.	Get a palaeontologist to come to our class.
The biggest dinosaurs were herbivores.	How much did they eat a day?	Dinosaurs lived on land and in the sea.	
Crocodiles are modern-day dinosaurs.	Were crocodiles alive when dinosaurs lived?	There are lots of very old things that still live in the sea.	
A meteor did something that killed the dinosaurs.	How did the dinosaurs really die?	The ice age came because smoke blocked out the sun.	Get out a DVD about climate change.

Brainstorming

Brainstorming is a very useful procedure for highlighting students' prior knowledge and/or developing creative solutions to a problem. It is a great way of challenging established routines or patterns of thinking in order to see new ways of looking at things. As a whole class activity, brainstorming can be used to bring out a range of students' ideas. It is important that students are able to express their ideas without being judged so there should be no criticism of students' ideas. The better this is done, the richer and more honest the ideas and solutions are likely to be. Brainstorming is a lateral thinking process and encouraging lateral ideas and thoughts is the real point of the exercise. But, in so doing, brainstorming also helps teachers to see what their students are thinking and/or understand before embarking on a topic or solving a problem. Brainstorming works well when:

- the problem/topic is clearly defined;
- a strong focus on the problem/topic is maintained;
- there is no criticism or evaluation of ideas during the session;
- no one person dominates for too long; and
- students develop others' ideas, not just their own.

Think–Pair–Share

There are many ways in which this teaching procedure can be adapted and used. In terms of drawing out students' prior knowledge, the 'think' component is most important at the individual level. Pairing allows students to compare and contrast their ideas in a one-to-one situation before sharing and further refining their ideas in a larger group.

Think is an individual brainstorming activity whereby students construct a list of their ideas or knowledge about the topic. This should be completed in a fixed period of time (approximately five minutes).

Pair is when two students work together in order to talk through their ideas and to construct one common list that they can then take to a larger group.

Share is when a number of pairs combine. Three pairs combined makes a good sharing group, but this will vary depending on total class size. Lists are compared with the purpose of refir ing ideas gathered on one common list.

By asking students at the end of a Think–Pair–Share session to reflect on their initial ideas and how they have (or have not) changed through the pairing and sharing, it helps to highlight for them how difficult it can sometimes be to shift their original ideas about a topic. This experience can be a helpful reminder for students to pay more careful attention to what they are supposed to be learning.

Anticipation reaction guide

The anticipation reaction guide (see Table 4.2) is specifically designed to get an overview of students' knowledge before and after a lesson. Like the KWLH, this procedure also works very well for text analysis.

Table 4.2 Anticipation reaction guide

Prior knowledge topic survey: Anticipation reaction guide		
Instructions: Respond to each of the statements below twice: first before the lesson and then again after it. Write **A** if you *agree* with the statement. Write **D** if you *disagree* with the statement.		
Response **BEFORE**	**TOPIC**: Immunology	Response **AFTER**
	There are diseases where your body fights against itself.	
	Vaccines are dead versions of the disease they fight against.	
	You can't catch the same disease twice.	
	A transplanted organ can reject the body it is transplanted into.	
	All bacteria are deadly.	
	Viruses can live in the Arctic.	
	Bacteria die if they are boiled.	

An important feature of the anticipation reaction guide is the reflective focus incorporated through responding to each of the statements, firstly before the lesson and then again after.

Semantic map

Semantic maps are constructed individually or in a group. They are a very useful way of helping students to organise their thinking and compare it to the thinking of others. As a way of bringing out students' prior views, semantic maps work very well at the start of a unit of work. A semantic map is organised with the central theme or idea placed in the middle, and then relevant categories (from three to five) radiate out from that point. Students are asked to make a bullet-point list with as many things as they know or think about on the topic being recorded. As with brainstorming it is important that students do not feel judged in recording their ideas or that there are correct ideas to be written down. This is important so that students can better link the new information with their existing ideas/prior knowledge.

Jo Osler and Jill Flack (2008) have used semantic maps extensively with primary school classes and have found them to be a productive way of helping students recognise and respond to their own and their classmates' prior knowledge. They note that:

> Our experience tells us that many students are unaware of the wealth of knowledge that they bring to any learning situation. We discovered that students benefit from explicitly acknowledging what it is they know that is connected to what they need to know. Semantic maps . . . support students to better organise their prior knowledge. Using keywords helps them think about the topic and to sort out what they already know . . . we augment semantic maps by providing opportunities for discussion to promote further thinking. Semantic maps can also be used to show new learning. Students can list what they know in one colour and, as they learn more, they can come back and 'top up' their semantic map in another colour. We've found that before we even use semantic maps it is best to share some experiences related to the topic under consideration . . . In some cases there are students who have little knowledge

about, or no personal experience of, the topic. Therefore, by giving students a shared experience, they all have something to draw on and share. (Osler & Flack, 2008: 26)

The example in Figure 4.8 is taken from one of Osler and Flack's Year 5/6 classes. It is a recreation of a class semantic map generated from their study of ants.

Figure 4.8 Semantic map: Ants

The Frayer model

The Frayer model is a graphic organiser that is a little like a semantic map with a defined structure. It has the main concept at the centre surrounded by four compartments for information related to that concept: essential characteristics; examples; non-essential character-istics; and non-examples. The Frayer model encourages students to draw on their existing knowledge to determine what is important for completing the task. An example is given in Figure 4.9.

Figure 4.9 Frayer model: Vegetables

Essential characteristics	Non-essential characteristics
• are a nutritious food • contain vitamins & minerals • come from non-woody plants • are a direct part of a plant: stem, leaf, bulb, root, tuber, seed or fruit	• colour • which part of plant is eaten • whether they grow above or below ground • whether they are eaten raw or cooked • size • planted from seeds
VEGETABLES	
Examples	Non-examples
• beans • carrots • cucumbers • potatoes • squash • radish • lettuce • herbs? • watermelon? • strawberries?	• tree fruit, such as apples, cherries, oranges • mushrooms • sugar, honey, maple syrup • woody vine plants such as grapes • woody cane plants such as raspberries

Source: adapted from Buehl, 2001: 57

Overview

This chapter was designed to explore the notion of prior knowledge and to situate it within the language and practice of teaching and learning. It has demonstrated how prior knowledge impacts learning and why prior knowledge needs to be carefully considered in relation to how we approach our teaching. The term prior knowledge carries substantial common-sense meaning and should be regarded as a central element of a language of teaching and learning that can help to inform and direct practice.

5
Processing

As teachers and learners we are all familiar with situations in which we recognise that we know something, but do not really understand that information enough to know how to explain it or use it in other situations. For example, science students often rote learn the definition of osmosis and, despite being able to recite it word for word, struggle to explain how osmosis is different from diffusion or why osmosis is an important function in living organisms. More so, when challenged by different examples of the movement of substances across a membrane, despite knowing the definition, for many choosing that which is and is not an example of osmosis proves to be very difficult. When it comes to explaining the concept of osmosis in relation to the real world, having the definition alone is not enough. This problem of students learning school science but not genuinely understanding the concepts is an ongoing challenge for science teachers.

In a similar way, history teachers sometimes struggle to get students to move beyond seeing history as a series of dates and events, just as language teachers are often confronted by students who can expertly recite terms and phrases when triggered to do so but struggle when the cue or question is slightly changed from that which they normally encounter. Therefore, there is a clear difference between knowing information and being able to apply it in different ways and situations. Assisting students to move beyond just knowing the information is important and is at the heart of teachers' professional knowledge of practice. Teaching for understanding is putting that professional knowledge into action in classrooms in thoughtful and meaningful ways.

Teaching for understanding requires propositional knowledge (such as facts, definitions and information) to be developed and used by learners in ways that go beyond simply absorbing the information and regurgitating it when asked to do so, most commonly through low-level assessment tasks. Absorption and recitation of information is typically associated with surface learning and such an approach to learning can create problems when it becomes the major script for students' approaches to school learning. Therefore, changing the script enhances learning so that the particular knowledge under consideration might be more meaningful, relevant and useful for learners. For this to happen, the information must be processed. *Processing* means that the information is deconstructed, looked at from different perspectives and linked to existing knowledge and ideas so that it might be able to be used in different ways and appropriately applied in different situations.

Studies in psychology offer very strong evidence that:

> people's active mental processing operations form a powerful and important cause of learning and remembering. Of the many factors that influence what a person learns, none has a larger influence than the kinds of mental processing activities that are carried out by the learner, deliberately or otherwise, at the time the person is attending to the material or information that is to be learned. (Howe, 1999: 33)

In learning, processing matters because it is one way in which a learner can begin to impose a structure on the material. Processing can help a learner begin to organise information in ways that make sense so that it can be recalled and used appropriately when needed. Clearly, when information is stored in a meaningful way, it is able to be more easily retrieved and used in the future. By thinking about processing in this way, the difference between remembering and learning becomes immediately apparent and the value of processing as an activity emerges as an integral component of teaching and learning.

The differences between short-term and long-term memory

have been well documented (see Chapter 2). Short-term memory has been described as an initial or temporary storage space in which a small number of items might be saved (seven plus or minus two). This initial storage can be enhanced through repeating the information (recitation/rehearsal) and/or through chunking (related elements being 'chunked' together to form one unit). Long-term memory is the permanent storage space and has a seemingly unlimited capacity. There are three types of long-term memory: episodic (memories of events); procedural (procedures in performing a skill); and semantic (language related). Facilitating the movement of information from short-term to long-term memory is important and processing is one way of consolidating that shift. However, to make that shift is not necessarily as simple as it may sometimes appear.

We often carry large amounts of well-rehearsed or chunked information in our heads in ways that can be overwhelming for our students who are not so familiar with the particular information or ideas. In so doing, we may not necessarily recognise what seem to be well-linked, easily stored ideas and information to us can cause cognitive overload in our students—there is simply too much information to absorb and retain.

Processing, as an active element of learning, can be catalysed through teaching. When we think about what needs to be processed, and how and why, there is a greater possibility that the script for learning can change so that a meaning-making focus might displace a 'recitation and recall' focus. Thinking carefully about the ways in which processing can be encouraged through teaching approaches can assist students in shifting information from their short-term to their long-term memory because they develop a deeper purpose in that learning. Therefore, the level of processing (surface or deep) becomes important in embedding the learning in long-term memory in ways that allow it not only to be remembered but also to be useable in meaningful ways.

Surface processing is characterised by a lack of attention to detail, where analysis is largely superficial; skimming is a good example of surface processing. Deep processing, as the term suggests, is when full attention is paid to detail so that analysis leads to the creation of strong links to existing knowledge. Deep processing means that ideas and information are sorted and organised in ways that contribute to understanding. Teaching for understanding, therefore, is all about encouraging processing to move beyond the surface so that it becomes deeply embedded in a learner's long-term memory. To do so, a learner needs to pay attention, or *attend*, to the information in ways that will encourage processing. Attending can be viewed as occurring at different levels. White (1988) explains these levels through an example:

> Imagine a student reading a science text or listening to the teacher. The text or teacher transmits the message, 'black things radiate heat better than silver things'. At the lowest level, the student does not select this event for attention at all, and it does not get into the short-term memory. Everyone has experienced this level of attention: you have been listening, then you are distracted, and when you return to the message some time later you are aware that the speaker must have been talking for some time but you have no idea at all of what has been said. In reading one can keep looking at the book but one's thoughts take over and prevent selection of the words, which are no longer 'seen'.
>
> At the next level, the words are selected and translated into meaningful forms and get into the short-term memory, but are not processed further. They are buried by succeeding words. The student reads, in the sense of decoding the printed symbols into words, but cannot tell what they were about. This too, is a common experience: one reaches the end of a page and is about to turn over, when one realises that the words have made no impression; or one is aware that the teacher is speaking, without being able to recall more than the most immediate words.
>
> The third level involves some processing, usually imaging of terms without the establishment of a large network of links to other propositions and episodes. The learner hears or sees the words, and checks out that 'black things' and 'radiate heat' and so forth make sense, but does not go as far as thinking about applications of the principle or evaluating it.
>
> The fourth level refers to deep processing, where all of the acts of linking, explaining and evaluating are carried out.
>
> The fifth and last level is where, in addition, the learner is in full

conscious control of the processing, and can extend or complete it at will. It involves the cognitive strategy of determining the purpose of the learning. (White, 1988: 153–4)

Attending and processing, therefore, go hand in hand in learning. However, learning—including processing and the level to which it is attended—is not simply controlled by these cognitive functions. Learning is also influenced by the way we feel (the affective domain) and how we share and interact in our learning with others (the social domain). Teaching for understanding draws on the cognitive, affective and social to transform learning into a meaningful act that is expertly designed and organised. Quality in teaching is when activities, procedures and strategies are developed and used by teachers to encourage selection, attending and processing. Teachers' professional knowledge is clearly evident in how they carefully plan and implement teaching approaches that encourage deep processing. Quality in teaching is not about using a teaching procedure just to break up the normal classroom routine; it is about using a particular teaching approach for a particular reason. There is a pedagogic intent that is closely tied to the professional knowledge of practice and how that can be used to enhance students' learning.

Teaching procedures: Processing

Jumbled text
For this teaching procedure, a page of text (usually no more) is cut up so that each paragraph is a separate block of text. Students are then asked to read the text and arrange the paragraphs in order so that the information makes sense. Introducing a diagram or picture into the text can add another level to the activity, as can combining this procedure with the one above (creating headings/sub-headings). Figure 5.1 below provides an example of a jumbled text.

Pyramids
Students are asked to read through the paragraphs outlined in Figure 5.1 then arrange them in the order that they think works best for explaining the story.

Figure 5.1 Jumbled text: Pyramids

1   When the pyramid was almost finished, a special block covered in shining metal (either gold or electrum) was placed on the top of the pyramid. Then, blocks of white limestone from quarries across the Nile were used to cover the pyramid. The blocks were trimmed to make the outside of the pyramid smooth. Finally, the pyramid was finished.

2   They planned a large pyramid—the largest one ever built in ancient Egypt. The outlines of the pyramid were measured and marked in the desert sand.

3   For about twenty years, hundreds of men worked on building the pyramid. As they built each level, they also built up the ramps around the pyramid.

4   Then the building began. Large blocks of stone were cut from quarries nearby. They were dragged by groups of men across the desert to the site of the pyramid and set in place. Most of the workers were farmers who worked on building the pyramid during the flood season when their fields were under water.

5   Khufu's pyramid was only part of the complex built for him at Giza. This complex had many different parts:
   • Three pyramids for Khufu's queens.
   • Several deep pits containing boats that had been buried.
   • A mortuary temple where Khufu would be worshipped after he died.
   • A causeway leading from the pyramid complex down to the valley temple.
   • A valley temple where the pharaoh's funeral would begin.
   • A small 'satellite' pyramid.
   • The mastaba tombs of nobles.

6   Khufu's architects were wise and experienced men. They knew the importance of building the pharaoh's final resting place so that its sides faced directly north, south, east and west.

7   After the first level of blocks was in place, the workers built ramps of mud brick, limestone chips and clay. The workers dragged the large stones up the ramps to build the next level of the pyramid.

8   The pharaoh Khufu, like the pharaohs before him, began planning his 'house of eternity' as soon as he took the throne. A spot was chosen for building on the west bank of the Nile. Cemeteries were usually built on the west bank because the sun 'died' on the western horizon every night.

Source: © *Trustees of the British Museum*

Students can check their story and see pictures of the building of the pyramid at the British Museum website: <www.ancientegypt.co.uk/pyramids/home.html>.

Creating headings/sub-headings

With this teaching procedure, students are given a block of text with the headings and sub-headings removed. They are asked to read the text and to then create their own headings and sub-headings. The procedure is designed to encourage students to process the information in such a way that the headings and sub-headings they create are good indicators of the theme of the text that follows. Further processing can also be encouraged by asking students to paraphrase the text into bullet points.

Question grid

Using this teaching procedure, students might work alone, in pairs or in small groups to complete a question grid. The question grid could be based on the topic being studied; for example, frogs, a particular book or other forms of information. The students write the questions that they have as a result of thinking about the information. The categories on the left of the grid can help students start to think about how they organise their learning about the topic. Table 5.1 shows an example based on frogs.

Table 5.1 Question grid: Frogs

Why?	Why are frogs green?	
When?	When do frogs mate?	
How?	How long do frogs live?	
Who?	Who studies frogs?	
Where?	Where do frogs live?	
What?	What do frogs eat?	

Information grid

In a similar vein to the question grid, this teaching procedure encourages students to think more deeply about particular aspects of the information they are studying; for example, characters in a story. It helps them to process particular information and to categorise that information in ways that encourage them to compare and contrast particular elements in an organised and structured manner. The example in Table 5.2 is based on the story 'Jack and the Beanstalk'.

Table 5.2 Information grid

Character	Physical description	Special words used	Special activities
Giant	Very large person	Fee-fi-fo-fum	Sleeping

Question dice

This teaching procedure is based on asking questions about particular information in ways that are determined by the roll of the dice. Question dice comprise a pair. The first die should have one of WHO, HOW, WHAT, WHY, WHEN/WHERE, WHICH on each of the six faces. On the second die, choose from IS, DID, DOES, CAN, WOULD, WILL, COULD, MIGHT for each face. An example can be seen in Figure 5.2. Having read the text or completed studying the topic, the question dice are used as a way of forcing processing. Students roll the dice and have to ask a question using the stem created by the dice; for example, 'What would . . .', 'How might . . .', 'Why does . . .', and so on.

Many variations for using question dice are possible. The teacher could roll the dice and propose the stem to the class to construct a question, or students could roll the dice and seek responses to the stem, or it could be done in groups so that questions (and answers) could be compared, or the first student to create a question could assume control of the dice, and so on.

Figure 5.2 Question dice

Analysing a picture/poster

As the name suggests, this teaching procedure involves using a picture or a poster as the source of information to be analysed. Students are asked to look at the image and to make statements or write questions about the things that capture their attention or that they wish to know more about. By using this teaching procedure, different forms of content can be analysed and students can see that information exists in forms other than text.

Grids

This teaching procedure uses chunks of information from a theme or topic and places them in a grid. Students are then asked to determine which chunks (in cells 1 to 15) help to answer the question(s). Variations on the grids could involve using pictures or diagrams instead of text, or asking students in small groups to construct the information for the grids and to write a couple of questions for other members of the class to answer.

Table 5.3 illustrates how a 'chunking' grid might be constructed and used with a class studying the British agricultural revolution.

Table 5.3 Example of a 'chunking' grid

1 In the 1730s Charles Townsend improved agricultural procedures by crop rotation.	2 In 1733 John Kay invented the flying shuttle, which increased the speed of the weaving process.	3 Population growth in the 1700s led to a shortage of cloth as the domestic system could not meet the demand for supply.
4 The industrial revolution produced a new social class of industrial workers.	5 Jethro Tull invented the seed drill.	6 Farmers in Britain began to grow new crops from the Americas such as potatoes and corn during the 1700s.
7 In the early 1700s Thomas Newcomen developed a steam-powered pump.	8 In 1785 Edmund Cartwright built a power loom powered by water which increased cloth production by 200 times.	9 Farmers who lost their land drifted to the towns in search of work.
10 Increased food production during the 1700s contributed to rapid population growth.	11 The enclosure movement fenced off public lands in the 1700s.	12 Between 1840 and 1850 the British built over 5000 miles of railway tracks.
13 Farming methods became more efficient, meaning fewer people were needed to work the land.	14 In the 1500s and 1600s rural families made cloth in their own cottages. This was part of the domestic system.	15 During the 1700s iron ploughs replaced less efficient wooden ploughs.

List the numbers from the grid that help to explain:
the agricultural revolution in Britain.
how the agricultural revolution made the industrial revolution possible.

Source: adapted from Mitchell & Mitchell, 1997: 15

Fact file

The fact file is a teaching procedure that has been well explained by Jo Osler and Jill Flack in their book *Whose learning is it?: Developing children as active and responsible learners* (2008). As very experienced teachers, Osler and Flack illustrate how a fact file can be used to 'invite students to visually display in poster form what they know, without having to write huge amounts of notes . . . it allows students to communicate their developing knowledge and understanding . . . information is displayed on one page and smaller chunks of researched facts/information are pasted onto the sheet after they have been drafted' (Osler & Flack, 2008: 69).

Figure 5.3 illustrates the outcome of this procedure from a Grade 3 student working on spiders.

Figure 5.3 Fact file: Spiders

Source: Osler & Flack, 2008

Writing on the reading

This teaching procedure is an excellent way of helping students avoid superficial processing. Writing on the reading involves students reading the text carefully in order to interrogate the information and ideas in ways that are not so common when simply skimming the information. The example in Figure 5.4 demonstrates how this procedure can encourage students to attend to and process information more deeply.

Figure 5.4 Writing on reading

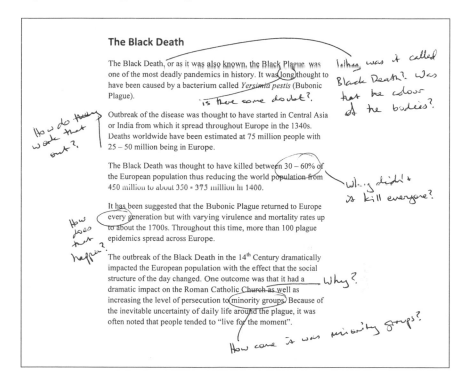

Plus–Minus–Interesting (PMI)

This teaching procedure is a good processing activity, especially so for decision-making processes. It works well by holding back on action and reconsidering the positive, negative and interesting aspects of the situation before making a decision about what to do, particularly if the decision-making is meant to be directed towards improvement in the situation. The procedure could be applied to students' own decisions about ideas or actions, but is equally valuable for considering the decisions of others, for example, characters in a story.

The PMI grid, as seen in Table 5.4, comprises three columns

(Plus, Minus, Interesting). As the terms suggest, in the Plus column students write down all the positive aspects of taking the action. In the Minus column they write down the negative effects. In the Interesting column they note all the implications and likely outcomes of taking the action, regardless of being positive, negative or unsure.

Table 5.4 Plus–Minus–Interesting (PMI) grid: Mummification

Plus	Minus	Interesting
Preserved for the afterlife	Pulled brain out through the nose	Takes 70 days to dry out a body

Overview

This chapter provided an overview of the notion of processing, situating it within the language and practice of teaching and learning. From the examples, we can see how important processing is for creating meaningful ways of enhancing learning so that knowledge construction might extend beyond the simple accumulation of information. In so doing, there is an expectation that learners will be more actively engaged in pedagogic experiences.

6
Linking

Linking is making connections across ideas so that prior knowledge and new knowledge can interact in ways that will further develop a student's understanding of the topic being studied. Jo Osler and Jill Flack have developed an interesting aspect of their pedagogical expertise through helping their students to be more effective learners as a result of their focus on linking.

> Once we started to explore linking we found that our students made many links naturally; but their attempts to articulate them were generally ineffective. We found that in the beginning students were often reluctant to share the connections they were making, maybe as a result of previous experiences at school, where this had not been seen as quite so important. Once we convinced students that we were genuinely interested in their efforts to make links, they gradually began to offer them without our prompts or praise.
>
> In order for us to develop linking with our students we had to first identify the important components that we felt would enhance the learning for our students . . . Although over the years our approach to teaching linking has continued to develop, our list of understandings stayed fairly constant. We want our students to: realise that school is more than a series of unrelated episodes; see learning as 'building on'; and make personal connections by accessing their prior knowledge and linking it with new learning. (Osler & Flack, 2008: 19)

Although the idea of making links may seem simple and obvious, as Osler and Flack demonstrate in the quotation above, there is a big difference between thinking about links (to related ideas or events) and actually articulating meaningful links in ways that can inform learning of the particular topic under consideration. For example, we often experience the situation in class in which the questions we pose are responded to in ways that seem to bear little relevance to that which was asked. These 'red herrings' are usually linked in some way to the ideas being discussed but, unfortunately, the thinking underpinning those links may appear less than transparent to us as the teacher or the rest of the class. Developing students' abilities to link in meaningful ways is important in expanding the ways in which they understand a concept and, ultimately, how they can work with a concept in different situations and demonstrate that publicly to others.

Linking is a process that, in some instances, happens almost subconsciously. Something that happens in one context can be a reminder of a similar thing in another, and there are times when ideas spring to mind as a result of a series of links such that, in isolation, the beginning and end points themselves do not appear to be related, as in the notion of red herrings. Yet, when working through the links that have led from one point to another, the cascade of ideas and suggestions demonstrates well how complex linking can be and how, in some circumstances, unrelated events can be brought together to make sense of a situation.

Encouraging students to be effective linkers, and therefore more effective learners at school, can be a challenging task. It can be difficult because the routine of schooling can lead some students to develop a default learning mechanism based around minimising effort and maximising the required output only when they feel they need to—they can become conditioned to operate in ways that allow them to cope with the demands of schooling. Unfortunately, this means that they can become too expert at paying attention only to the immediate task or activity and inadvertently shun links to other knowledge, ideas, experiences and events that could enhance their learning. Therefore, a student's ability to link per se may not be a problem; rather, it might be the ability or motivation to do so under the normal conditions of schooling. This point has been demonstrated time and again throughout the research literature, which only goes to reinforce the importance of continually paying attention to the need to make linking explicit. Consider the following example, which could well be described as 'typical'.

Linking

[A] teacher was involved in a lesson where the effect of heat on the rate of dissolving of a potassium permanganate crystal in water at different temperatures was to be investigated. The teacher's perceptions of the context of the lesson were ... *this is the third lesson in a series aimed at developing a particle idea and going over the states of matter ... the first one (lesson) we did was also to do with this. It was to do with expansion and contraction of substances—today was a direct follow-on from that.*

The following pupil comment, however, was typical of the pupils' perceptions:

Observer: What was today's lesson about?

Robert: What crystals can do.

Observer: Does today's work have anything to do with this other work you have been doing (pointing to the pupil's open exercise book which was showing notes headed up as the 'dilution of a potassium permanganate crystal' and 'heating and expanding liquids')?

Robert: No, not really ... no.

What was an obvious and strong linkage of material from the teacher's point of view was not at all obvious to this pupil. (Osborne & Freyburg, 1985: 69)

The need to help students realise that school is more than a series of unrelated episodes is clearly important. Linking not only matters from lesson to lesson within a subject but also across subjects. With the wide range of content covered in classes it stands to reason that the more active a student is in making links, the easier it is to remember that content and therefore the more likely it is that richer understandings will eventuate.

Linking learning to episodes and events from students' own lives clearly helps to make learning more relevant and so the teacher should act as a catalyst for linking rather than directing the form that linking should take. Linking benefits from being student initiated, and is more likely to create greater personal meaning as the particular experiences, ideas, knowledge, episodes and events able to be linked to that content will vary enormously from student to student.

Making progress

As noted above, challenging students' default school-learning script requires them to recognise a need to make a change to the way they approach their learning. One way of doing that is through ensuring they experience a sense of making progress. In so doing, it is then more likely that the value of linking will be reinforced—and therefore become part of their learning routine.

Making progress means that students need to see advantages in trying to search for links. A good beginning point is through linking with personal experiences. We commonly remember the details of events in which we have been personally involved and it is through this personal connection that linking can become a powerful aid to learning. Making personal connections increases relevance for students and also *gives them permission* to think in different ways about the work they are doing. Students who study history but do not make links to their own experiences (related to the topic, place or events of the time, for example) may come to see history as a long list of facts and information to be remembered. However, students who do link the topic to their own experiences develop many more points of connection between that which is being learnt and that which they already know and so their learning is enhanced; so too is the likelihood that they will have a more positive attitude toward the topic being studied.

An important aspect of making links, and therefore progress in learning, is in the extent to which linking can be made public in order to facilitate the thinking of others, as opposed to remaining an individual and private process. When students are able to talk aloud about the connections they are making, not only is it helpful for them but it can also be helpful for others. Interestingly, the very process of making links in a public way can create a memorable episode for a class and, as a shared experience, can be another way of supporting students' learning through the personal connections they make as a result of that learning experience. For example, in a class discussion a link that one student makes to the topic may well trigger similar thinking by another. If students relate to others the given situation that they have experienced, it can create new links for other students and help to open up new ways of thinking about the topic that might not otherwise have been possible. Through these sorts of personal connections, meaning making is fostered and learning progresses beyond simply remembering information into ways of knowing that are much more intertwined and evocative. Through linking, many more effective avenues to explore the topic become possible.

Teaching procedures: Linking

What if . . .?

What if questions encourage students to think imaginatively, creatively and laterally about what they know. *What if* questions can be posed by the teacher or the students and can be based around classroom discussions, particular texts and/or posters, photographs or diagrams. In answering *what if* questions, students not only draw on their learning of the topic but also the links they make with their existing knowledge. Some examples are:

- What if the Governor–General had not dismissed the Whitlam Government in 1975?
- What if the earth's axis was on a tilt of more (or less) than its 23.5 degrees?
- What if the South had won the American Civil War?
- What if we ran out of oil?
- What if there had not been a gold rush?
- What if the wolf was good and Little Red Riding Hood was bad?

From there to here

This teaching procedure is designed to encourage students to make links between what they already knew and what they have learnt. It is therefore an effective procedure to use at varying times throughout a unit of work.

At the start of a unit it can be helpful to establish links to existing knowledge. During a unit it can be good for students to have some time-out to think about making more substantive links to the topic. At the end of a unit, linking is an excellent way of consolidating and reviewing that learning. Table 6.1 provides an example based on The Crusades.

Table 6.1 From there to here: The Crusades

What I knew	Links I made to get to ➤	What I know now ➤
Richard the Lion Heart was the 'good' King and Prince John was his 'wicked' brother.	Robin Hood was a big supporter of King Richard and the Sheriff of Nottingham was a big supporter of Prince John.	Prince John wasn't really that bad but the stories made him look bad. The story of Robin Hood tells a different story about Prince John to the real history. The Robin Hood story was built up over time from myths and legends. Not everything in it really happened.
Crusades to the holy land were about the English trying to recapture Jerusalem from the Muslims.	I have been to Jerusalem and seeing the city walls and the narrow streets made me think about how hard it would be to fight there. The city looks like I think it would have looked back then.	Crusaders made special vows and were given *indulgences* for sins they had done in the past. Not all crusades were against Muslims, they were also against Christians, as well as Jews, Pagans, Russians and Greeks.

Linking through a labelled diagram

By labelling a diagram students can demonstrate some of the key points that they know or have learnt about a topic. They can then extend their labelled diagram by expanding on that information by linking it to other aspects of the topic that they know about or are interested in questioning or knowing more about. Figure 6.1 shows an example of a labelled diagram of a castle.

Figure 6.1 A labelled diagram

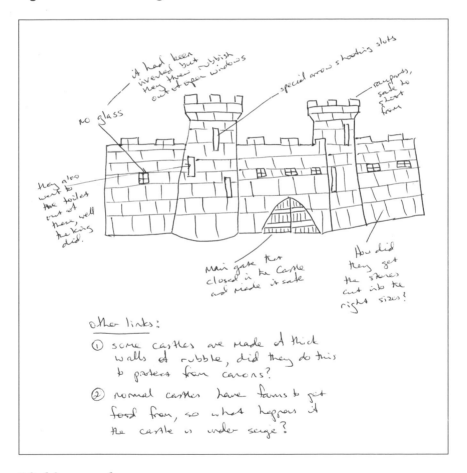

Linking cycle

This teaching procedure is particularly applicable to topics that include some form of cycle or flow of events. The linking cycle is used to show how a student understands the interactions in that cycle. Examples are: the life cycle of a frog; parts of a poem or story; making iron in a blast furnace; weather patterns or building a pyramid. The linking cycle shows how the ideas are linked together so that the whole concept is explained and understood in a coherent form. The important questions that frame how the students construct their cycle are:

1 What are the critical events in this cycle?

2 How are they related?

3 Why must they follow this order?

The linking cycle works best if the number of events is limited. About five events tend to be most manageable; more than that and the cycle can become too complex and cause a shift from a focus on linking to simply stating facts. Figure 6.2 provides an example.

Figure 6.2 The linking cycle

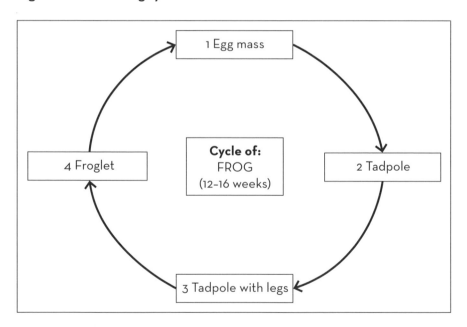

Linking very different parts of the work

This is a PEEL (Project for Enhancing Effective Learning, Baird & Mitchell, 1986; Baird & Northfield, 1992) teaching procedure that is able to be easily initiated at any time during a unit of work. The teacher selects two parts of the work that students have probably not attempted to link; of course, it is important that there is a relationship between the two parts so they are worth linking. The procedure is described as follows:

> Two broad types of links can be called for. One is between widely separated ideas, facts or concepts, e.g., can you see a link between the ideas on page 2 and page 85? In this case the teacher suspects that the ideas on pages 2 and 85 will not have been linked simply because they were presented several weeks apart. The second type of linking is between two different activities such as theory and practical work, practical work and numerical problems, or excursions and theory. For example: Where is this section of numerical problem 27 duplicated in experiment 8? Where on the excursion did we see an application of the idea on page 13? (Mitchell, 2007: 13)

Linking to real life

This teaching procedure is designed to encourage students to link what they are learning to examples from the real world. It works best when the examples are drawn from students' own life experiences.

Students are asked to write in their own words any links that they can make between the content they have been studying and their own everyday experiences; for example, 'surveying is a data-gathering technique that is used extensively in the social sciences'. Many students will have experienced telemarketers calling them at home in an attempt to gather information, or they may have been interviewed on a street corner by market researchers with their clipboards and interview protocols. Linking the idea of data and the results of that analysis with data-collection techniques that they may have experienced is one way of helping them to begin to think about the pros and cons of such procedures. Another example is in the process of recycling. Students may be well aware of products developed as a consequence of recycling but not link these to their own efforts (or not) of separating the disposable and recyclable articles in their own rubbish.

Sweller questions

Sweller questions are designed to encourage students to find out everything they can about a particular situation. As a consequence they are free to link information and ideas in ways that they think are appropriate to help explain the situation or solve the problem. Sweller questions have been extensively used in mathematics. A typical example would be to present students with a geometric-shaped object (for example, a cardboard box) and ask them to calculate as many things as they can about the object. They might calculate its volume, surface area, perimeters, diagonals and so on. Completing the task in pairs or small groups is a very helpful way of bouncing ideas off one another, further reinforcing the linking of, in this case, algorithms and their appropriate application and use.

Creating analogies

In this teaching procedure students are asked to think about the concept that they have been studying and to develop an analogy for that concept that they think will stand up well to scrutiny. For example, an analogy for the circulatory system might be the public transport system, or in the case of electricity moving in a circuit, an analogy might be water moving through a hose. Analogies are helpful in linking abstract ideas to concrete examples but in most cases the analogy eventually breaks down. Ensuring that students can not only develop analogies but also recognise their limitations is important.

Synectics

W.J.J. Gordon (1961) introduced the idea of synectics as a way of encouraging imaginative thinking and creating new ways into a problem. It can be particularly helpful when beginning a creative writing exercise or for looking differently at something. Synectics can be used to make the strange familiar, or the familiar strange.

Synectics is based on the use of analogy or metaphor and helps students to challenge their existing mindset and internalise abstract concepts. The procedure for synectics is as follows:

1 *Describe the topic:* The teacher selects a word or topic and asks

students to describe it, either in small group discussions or by individually writing a paragraph; for example, apples.

2 *Create direct analogies:* The teacher selects another word or topic (for example, rocks) and asks the students to generate a list of things that have the same characteristics as those created in Step 1; for example, 'How are apples and rocks alike?' Creating a visual is very helpful at this point.

3 *Describe personal analogies:* Students then select one of the direct analogies and create their own personal analogy by imagining being the object chosen and describing what it feels like. For example, 'How would it feel to be an apple that feels like a rock?'

4 *Identify compressed conflicts:* Students then pair words from the list generated in Step 3 that conflict with one another and explain that link. Students choose one pair and work with it. For example, 'How are fruit and animals different?'

5 *Create a new direct analogy:* Students then create a different direct analogy by choosing something that is described by the paired words. For example, 'How are fruit and animals like a poem, a sporting event or a film?'

6 *Re-examine the original topic:* Students go back to the original idea and construct a description based on the ideas generated in the synectics process.

Thinking hats

The 'six thinking hats' (DeBono, 1992) is a framework that uses different coloured hats to represent six modes of thinking. They are directions to think rather than labels for thinking.

1 *The white hat* covers facts, figures and information and is about looking at the data.

2 *The red hat* represents intuition, feelings and emotions.

3 *The black hat* is for judgement and pointing out why a suggestion does not fit the facts.

4 *The yellow hat* is used to consider why something will work and for looking forward to the results and seeing the value in actions.

5 *The green hat* is for creativity, considering alternatives and thinking about new ideas and change.

6 *The blue hat* is the overview hat, and is for thinking about the thinking, that is, metacognition.

Mind maps

Mind maps are organised around a central theme or main idea, which is placed in the middle of the page. With the main theme in mind, students then brainstorm ideas connected to that theme. Ideas suggested by students should be one or two words only and are added to the page by radiating out from the original word or from the subsequent words.

A mind map is a form of graphic organiser that works very well at the beginning of a topic as it draws on students' prior knowledge and can help to set the scene for the work that is to follow. Mind maps can also form the basis of a good revision exercise.

Although a mind map might look like a concept map there are some important differences. A mind map does not have a list of supplied concepts to be used; it only has a central term (see Figure 6.3). The mind map develops strong visual representation based around the central idea being discussed to illustrate how other things relate to that idea. A mind map does not have the relationships between concepts noted on the connections between terms. Another aspect of a mind map is that it represents not only the main topic but also some of the sub-themes within these topics.

Tony Buzan (2002) has written extensively on mind maps and suggests some guidelines for mind map construction:

1 Start with a coloured image in the centre of the page.

2 Use images throughout your mind map.

3 Words should be printed.

4 The printed words should be on lines, and each line should be connected to other lines.

5 Words should be in units of one per line, allowing each word to have free hooks and giving more freedom and flexibility.

6 Use colours to enhance memory, delight the eye and stimulate the right cortical processes.

7   The mind should be left as free as possible. Students will prob-
    ably think of ideas faster than they can write.

Figure 6.3 Mind map: Wool

Overview

This chapter explored the notion of linking in the context of the
language and practice of teaching and learning. It has demonstrated
the importance of linking in storing, structuring and retrieving ideas,
knowledge and information and why it is crucial to high-quality
pedagogy.

7
Translation

Translation occurs when ideas and information presented in one way are processed and then used in another form. It requires cognitive manipulation as the ideas and information being worked with need to be well understood in order for them to be applied in a different way in a different setting.

Being able to translate information is one way for students to demonstrate a deeper understanding of a subject because the work of translation depends on much more than just restating facts and information. In many ways, translation is about tapping into our long-term memory and using the basis of our understanding of a given concept, idea, issue or theme in a different context.

In thinking about translation in terms of a psychological construct, the process is largely automatic and therefore not always within our conscious control. This is because, in most cases, what we know influences what we see or what we think we see. At one level, translation is evident through the way in which words on a page carry meaning for a reader. The brain takes the text and translates the arrangement of letters (looks for the patterns and sequences) so that they are able to be assembled in a way that makes sense to us. The process of translation becomes conscious when it does not happen automatically. For example, in situations in which we are confronted by an arrangement of letters that do not make sense or do not fit the patterns with which we are familiar, translation from text to meaning becomes difficult or does not occur at all. This is most apparent when observing forms of writing with which we are unfamiliar. For example, Thai script has different characters to English letters and there are no spaces between words. Spaces in a Thai text indicate the end of a clause or sentence. When we do not recognise particular shapes, patterns or sequences it is difficult to make sense of the information, while somebody familiar with the script immediately translates the text into meaning—hence, what we know influences what we see.

Another way of thinking about how translation occurs is in terms of the constructions we make of the world we see. It is not difficult to quickly recognise physical features of a landscape with which we are familiar, the various outlines of vegetation, landforms and animals do not usually require a great deal of effort to translate into familiar forms—even from a quick glance. However, in a new and different environment it can sometimes take quite careful observation and deliberate thinking to translate features into recognisable forms—or in some cases, no sense can be made of the forms at all.

Translation is affected not only by familiarity, but also by expertise:

> Knowledge affects sensation, so teacher and student may organise the stimuli they receive in different ways, and so may experience different sensations even when in the same surroundings. They may even see different things when looking from the same vantage point in the same direction. Thus, the student may see no more than an undifferentiated field of grass, while the geologist, or botanist, sees it as a number of highly contrasted areas, sharply defined. The difference between what skilled and unskilled observers see can be dramatic. (White, 1988: 126)

In a teaching and learning context, when knowledge and its application is required to help explain or make sense of a situation, translation as a process really begins to stand out as important. The significance stems from two different aspects of learning. The first is in translation being conducted as a conscious and explicit cognitive function. The second is through translation as a way of demonstrating understanding of information, ideas or concepts, and the ability to extend that through new and different forms or contexts. To translate, then, means the learner must make an effort—it is not a passive activity.

From thinking to doing: Active learning

As has been noted above, our minds perform translation activities subconsciously in order to quickly and effectively make sense of such things as our environment, episodes and events. Making the shift from a subconscious to a conscious act involves helping students recognise that translation is a process and then encouraging them to actively and overtly develop ways of using that process in their own learning. For that to be the case, students need to learn how to review or reconsider that which they know about the topic, concept or idea being studied (which is based around ideas of metacognition—see Chapter 9) in order to be able to determine the key elements needed in applying that idea in a different way. To do this is not a simple task and so translation activities create an expectation that students will be active learners.

Working with ideas in one context then using them in another can mean that students need to be adept at shifting their thinking between the concrete and the abstract. As is illustrated in the teaching procedures that follow, being able to manipulate concepts in an abstract form encourages students to think more deeply about what they know and how to apply it. In terms of teaching for understanding, cognitive manipulation is something that can be initiated but not necessarily controlled by the teacher. The process of translation occurs in different ways in different individuals depending on such things as their prior knowledge, the ways in which they process the information, and the particular links they are able to make to ensure that the process is meaningful as opposed to being a routine task.

This meaning-making is a crucial process of learning because it ultimately shapes the quality of the learning, and the individual learner controls that process. Therefore, if as teachers we try to direct the way that the process of translation should occur it would most likely be counterproductive as it would probably encourage students to respond as though it were a routine task—and therefore invoke default school-learning approaches.

One obvious value in implementing teaching procedures that are based around translation activities is that although the beginning and end points can be established by the teacher, the paths between are rightly able to be controlled and directed by the learner. Therefore, meaning making becomes a much more personally significant process and so is more likely to have a lasting influence on what the learner learns.

Pedagogy: The relationship between teaching and learning

In outlining his 'Principles of teaching for quality learning', Mitchell (2007: 184) draws attention to the idea of 'sharing intellectual control with students'. Sharing intellectual control means building a sense of shared ownership in order to encourage high levels of student interest and engagement. It means that students' questions, issues, ideas and comments are regularly used to shape what is done in a lesson. In order to share intellectual control, our thinking about pedagogy must come to the fore because the interactions between teaching and learning cannot be solely directed from one perspective (either the teacher's or the students').

Pedagogy is the relationship between teaching and learning and so it stands to reason that shared ownership is an effective way into that relationship. Translation activities create possibilities for such openings to be grasped and therefore create real opportunities for students to be engaged in their learning.

Jeff Northfield is of the view that quality learning requires learner consent—teachers cannot do the learning for their students. Therefore, developing creative and engaging ways of inviting students into learning is an important aspect of encouraging them to accept responsibility for their own learning. Northfield developed this view because he recognised that:

> Throughout the years of schooling, students develop their own views about what to expect from certain situations. They learn how to act and respond to a variety of stimuli. Their responses are not always in the form of behaviours which will assist them in learning, but they commonly help them to cope with the 'routine' demands of school. Therefore, their prior experiences are crucial in shaping their learning behaviour and, sadly, often do not fit the learning demands expected. This is particularly highlighted when the learning demands require students to make an effort and to take risks to further their understanding ... as a result of the accumulation of

experiences that do not actively encourage quality learning, it is not uncommon for students to rarely experience genuine understanding of the content being taught, hence they do not tend to link understanding with learning, so they do not expect to learn with understanding. All they need is to 'know' the work.

The idea that learning requires learner consent then is obvious, but it is most difficult to achieve. It clearly requires independence on the part of the student. (Loughran & Northfield, 1996: 123–4)

Creating pedagogic situations in which students operate as active learners is crucial to challenging their default school-learning routines. Translation activities are one way of unsettling these routines and 'forcing' students to think differently about what they are doing so that learning for understanding is not just encouraged but purposefully developed by the students.

Teaching procedures: Translation

Story from a graph/graph from a story

Translation activities are structured in such a way as to take information in one form and turn it into another. Graphs are a form of representation of information. Some students are very good at translating graphs into words or vice versa, but it is not all that common for such a translation process to be explicitly performed as a teaching procedure. Writing a story from a graph or making a graph from a story is one way of opening up this skill to students in an engaging and productive manner.

The name of this teaching procedure describes what happens. Students are asked to write a story from a graph. For example, they could write the story from a graph that shows the progress of a swimmer in a race or fluctuations in the stock market. The reverse of this process, graph from a story, also extends and develops graphing skills, and for some this can be a more difficult translation activity than working the other way (that is, story from a graph). In this case, students are given a text that outlines a particular set of events over time and are then asked to construct a graph to represent the changes that occur in the story.

The following example from the Mathematics Curriculum Teaching Package (MCTP) (Lovitt & Clarke, 1998) forms the basis of the story from a graph translation activity. Each of the lines in Figure 7.1 represents a coloured car at a particular part of a road over a particular period of time. Students are asked to form small groups and discuss what they can see happening in the graph, then tell the story of one of the cars and what a passenger might have seen and done.

Figure 7.1 Story from a graph

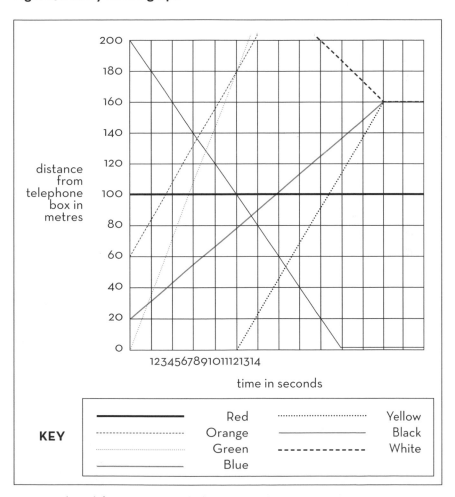

Source: adapted from Lovitt & Clarke, 1998: 256

Role-play

Role-playing is a very familiar form of translation activity. Typically this would involve a student playing a person in a particular situation that is based on events central to a theme or topic being studied, such as a novel or a play. A variation on this that takes translation to another level is when students are asked to role-play a process that is not quite so easy to observe or understand; for example, mitosis, machinery in action or electricity in a circuit.

It is important that students consider carefully what they do in the role-play so that the detail of the particular parts are adequately portrayed and that the difficulties or particular issues with the content are demonstrated in a reasonable way throughout. A helpful addition to the work of role-play is to assign a group of observers to document and critique the actions of the players and to raise questions about particular aspects of the work.

Role-plays that help students move from the abstract to the concrete or vice versa can be particularly powerful, as demonstrated by the following commentary on the role-play of the dark side of the Moon.

Learning to make the abstract concrete

One session that is vividly etched in my mind was the time I decided to use a role-play that I hadn't used before. I had noticed that in the past most of the role-plays only involved a small number of students and so I was conscious of the need to have more participants involved in doing things—and fewer students observing with no specified task to complete.

At the time, I was involved in a project that was documenting exemplary science teaching and so decided to use a role-play from that project that I knew would involve the whole class. On paper it was a good role-play. It ensured that all students did something and in our research group we had had some interesting discussions about the activity. Therefore, I felt relatively confident that I could successfully teach this particular role-play to my class.

The role-play was designed to explore the way the Moon

revolves around the Earth. I remembered that one of my colleagues had made a big point of the difference between the Moon *revolving* around the Earth as opposed to it *rotating* on its axis. It seemed a big point at the time, one of those 'scientific language' issues, so I was sensitised to something that was apparently an important learning point for my class.

I started off in the normal way by getting students' prior views, listing them on the board, pushing and probing their ideas and generally trying to create a sense of interest in the topic. The next phase was to set up the problem. This was not difficult either, it was something like: 'The Moon rotates on its axis once during its revolution of the Earth, so how is it that we only ever see the same face?' I'm not sure that before encountering this role-play I was ever aware of this myself (at least not beyond some esoteric link to my childhood and Pink Floyd's *Dark Side of the Moon*), so at first I think it probably made me stop and think, but not for too long as the problem was directed at the class (not me as the teacher). Besides, I was already fully occupied in teaching as I expertly stumbled through a teaching procedure that I usually did not like in a content area with which I was unfamiliar.

It finally dawned on me that we had to go outside if we were to have enough space to do the role-play—we would never manage the role-play in the confines of the classroom.

'Phew, some breathing space at last,' I thought as we meandered down the corridor on our way outside.

When we spread out under the oak trees, I quickly organised everybody into their positions. I knew it couldn't be too hard. All I needed was a small group of four or five students to make a circle by linking their arms while standing back to back—so that they would all be looking outwards. That group would be the Moon. Then the same formation was needed for the remainder of the students and they would be the Earth. So far, so good.

'Okay, Earth, start revolving (or should that be rotating?)'. A little quiver in my voice. I wondered if anyone noticed! 'Let's see how that goes,' I said. The role-play had begun.

It was a bit messy so I told the Earth to rotate a little more slowly. This was met by complaints about the pace of rotations necessary for them to manage a month in the time that the Moon would take to get back to its starting point—28 rotations.

'Hmm! I hadn't thought about that. Did it really matter?' I wondered to myself. 'You'll work something out,' I blithely responded.

'Now, Moon, start a revolution around the Earth, but while you do it, you have to organise yourselves to do only one rotation on your own axis. So, Janet, from where you are now, you need to be facing the Earth again when you get back to that spot. Put a mark on the ground so you know where that will be. Okay, off you go,' I said with great confidence.

I stood back and watched the role-play unfold. As the Moon slowly rotated in its revolution of the Earth I tried to visualise how it could be that if it rotated only once on its axis that only one side of the Moon would be seen from the Earth. I couldn't do it though. I just could not manipulate that in my mind to understand how it could be possible. But as I stood there watching it, I could see it happening before me. The abstract became very concrete.

When the Moon arrived back at its starting point I asked how the role-play had worked—I was now moving away from the prescribed script, with my curiosity piqued. Liz (a part of the Earth) and Athena (a part of the Moon) said they didn't get it. Having just watched it unfold before me, I decided that they would get it if they could see it happening so I got them to stand out and watch while we repeated the role-play and I took Athena's place in the Moon.

As the role-play unfolded again, I actually felt what it was like to be the dark side of the Moon and although I still couldn't really visualise what was happening, being a part of the action made it very real for me. Suddenly I got what it meant to be involved in a role-play. Suddenly I saw a number of important pedagogical insights. Suddenly content started to take new shape as a developing understanding slowly emerged. Suddenly our class became alive with learning, and I was part of it.

Together we pushed around ideas about teaching and learning as new and interesting insights into the nature of role-play became clear to all of us. Questions, issues and ideas about astronomy were also initiated and different role-plays were envisaged as the students discussed the fundamentals of this approach in relation to other topics such as summer and winter, and day and night.

After the class I mused over the episode again. I reflected on the previous weeks and how in the research group we had discussed this role-play when considering it for inclusion in the 'exemplary practice folder'. At the time, I was satisfied with my grasp of the ideas—I was certainly able to suggest advice for other teachers about how they could use the role-play and the value it offered as a teaching and learning tool. However, what I knew—or thought I knew—before the experience was dramatically different to what I knew after the experience. Being involved in the experience was different to directing it for others. Abstracting the learning from this experience to other situations was intellectually challenging and engaging. What I saw in my students' approach to learning was new and different. What I began to see in teaching was a revelation. What I previously knew, I now understood.

Although it appears obvious that understanding is enhanced through experience, it is curious how often in teaching information is substituted for experience. More so, although the value of experience is commonly acknowledged, there seems to be an implicit view that such experience is for the students, not the teacher. The vignette above illustrates how important experience is. Knowing about role-play was not sufficient—being a learner in a role-play created a situation in which new understandings of teaching were catalysed. (Loughran, 2006: 23-6)

Storyboarding (text to pictures)

Taken from its use in animations or films, storyboarding is a way of visualising and understanding the flow of main events or scenes in a story by laying them out in sequence. As a translation activity, storyboarding is a way of creating a visual layout of the content or information that is central to the theme or topic being studied.

Students can use storyboarding to develop their overview of a story as they think it could or should be told. An obvious extension is to consider the storyboard as the outline for a play, movie or animation (for example, slowmation).

Slowmation

Slowmation (abbreviated from 'slow animation') is a stop–motion process that dramatically simplifies the complex method of making animations so that they can be easily created by students of any age.

Slowmation involves the manual manipulation of materials with digital still photos taken as changes in the scenes are made, which are then played in sequence to create the illusion of movement (for a full explanation see Hoban, 2005). Students research information, develop a script, create a storyboard, design their models, digitally photograph their models between small manual movements, and use a computer program such as Apple QuickTime Pro or Windows Movie Maker to create the animation.

As slowmations are played slowly (two frames per second), learners are able to represent their own understandings in comprehensive ways and review what they have done. This translation activity can be applied across all subjects. For full details on the process and to view examples refer to Garry Hoban's web site: <http://edserver1.uow.edu.au/slowmation/>.

The still images in Figures 7.2 and 7.3 were created by a group of Grade 3 students. They show how scenes can be created with simple equipment and everyday props. Figure 7.2 illustrates the process of Egyptian mummification, while Figure 7.3 demonstrates an Olympic rowing event.

Fortune lines

Fortune lines are an interesting translation task that work very well for exploring feelings and emotions. They allow students to express ideas in graphical form in ways that are often easier than using words. Fortune lines are constructed using two axes. The vertical axis represents feelings or emotions and the horizontal axis is used to record events in time.

The events for a fortune line could be constructed by the teacher as a list of the important episodes derived from a story, text or piece of information, for example, or the students might construct their own list of events in terms of the things that they consider important in shaping the story. The following example is based on information about Marie Antoinette.

Figure 7.2 Slowmation: Pharaohs   **Figure 7.3 Slowmation: Rowing**

Maria Antonia Josepha Johanna von Habsburg-Lothringen (Marie Antoinette, 2 November 1755–16 October 1793)

1 Childhood: 1755–67

2 Married to Louis Auguste: 1767–70

3 Her husband is crowned King Louis XVI: 1775

4 First child born (girl): 19 December 1778

5 Miscarriage: 1779

6 Son born: 22 October 1781

7 Decrease in Marie Antoinette's popularity and power: 1782–85

8 Diamond necklace controversy: 1785–86

9 Propaganda suggested that she ruined France financially: 1786–89

10 French Revolution: 1789–92

11 King Louis executed: 21 January 1793

12 Marie Antoinette found guilty of treason: morning of 16 October 1793

13 Marie Antoinette executed in ordinary housewife's clothes: 12.15 p.m., 16 October 1793

Having constructed a fortune line, a student might then use it as the basis for writing a story of the events; the fortune line can then act as a reminder about aspects of the episodes that might otherwise not be drawn on in formulating their account. Figure 7.4 is a fortune line based on the above information about Marie Antoinette.

Model making

Making models can be a most enjoyable translation activity for students of all ages and is another way of helping students take abstract concepts and make them concrete, whether it be through the construction of an individual item, a diorama or a representation of the solar system, for example.

Extending the learning from model making can be encouraged by asking students to present their working model to others and/or to run a discussion and answer questions about the model in action.

Figure 7.4 Fortune line: Marie Antoinette

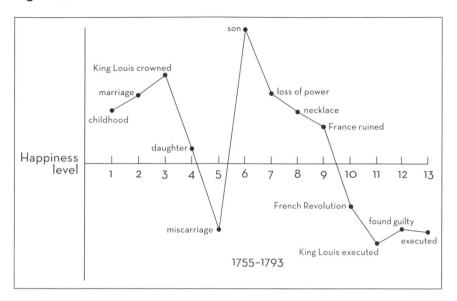

For some concepts (for example, a double helix of DNA, chemical compounds, a pyramid, bridge, beehive, ant nest or other physical feature), model construction can be a useful activity for helping to gauge students' understanding of the structure being represented.

A good example of how model making as a translation activity can assist students in moving between the abstract and concrete is in geography when thinking about the construction of a contour map. A contour map represents variations in land form and students can use something as simple as a potato to make the translation from one form (3-D topography) to another (2-D contour map).

Figure 7.5 Model making: Topography to contour

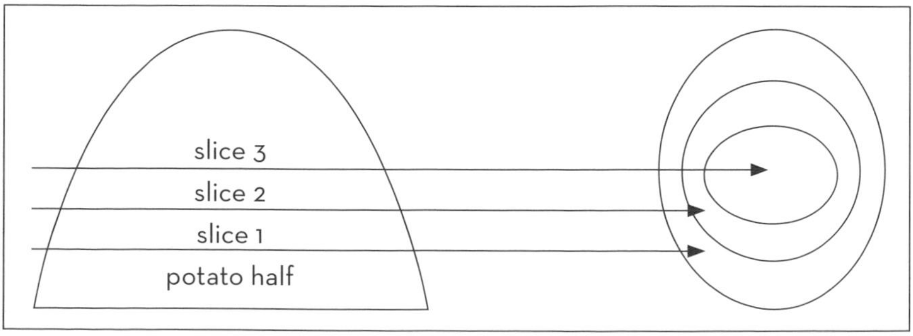

Students are asked to cut a potato in half and place one of the halves cut-side down on a piece of paper to represent a hill. They can see how a contour map is developed by slicing through the hill in horizontal layers and then laying out each piece and tracing around the outer edge one at a time, which quickly shows how the contours relate to the changes in topography (see Figure 7.5). In this way, students can see the 3-D feature grow into the graphic representation that is a contour map.

Creative writing

Creative writing is a translation task commonly used in the humanities to encourage students to think imaginatively and creatively, not only about what they know but also about what they are unsure of, or do not know, about a theme or topic. Hence, through the translation activity, students can begin to question their understanding of the topic in new ways.

Creative writing is perhaps less commonly used in the sciences but, as has been well demonstrated by the work of the McClintock Collective (1988), it can be a powerful way of helping students reconsider information and fill in gaps in their understanding as they translate ideas from one form to another. Consider, for example, how the following creative writing exercises might be completed by students:

1 Imagine you are a molecule of water. Describe your journey from the roots of a plant out into the atmosphere through transpiration. What would it be like? How would it feel? What changes might you see and/or experience on your journey?

2 If you were an apple, describe your journey through a human body following the first bite.

Writing a song or a poem

Turning one form of text into another can lead to very powerful learning through translation. Asking students to write a song or a poem based on work recently completed, or after reading a text or class discussion, can not only help them become more familiar with the structural features associated with that form of expression, but can also help them to consider more deeply the main issues and ideas necessary to demonstrate understanding of the topic.

Writing your own method

Writing your own method is a teaching procedure designed to help students think carefully about the steps that need to be undertaken to complete a particular procedure. In subjects that have a strong practical base it is not uncommon for students to approach the method or procedure for the activity without thinking about what they are doing or why. For example, in science laboratory practical work students can unthinkingly follow the method as a recipe without translating any of the purposes of the steps into deeper understandings of the theory supposedly being examined. One way to challenge this is to ask students to think carefully about the purpose or aim of the activity and to develop a procedure for conducting the activity. In this way students can be encouraged to link the theory and practical and to translate the ideas from one context into a concrete form in another.

An extension to this teaching procedure is to supply the equipment needed for the practical activity (perhaps even supply some equipment not needed for the task) and ask students to determine what to use and how to use it to satisfactorily answer the question or achieve the aim prescribed.

Graphs into action

This teaching procedure requires students to translate movement as depicted on a graph into action. The case on p. 120 by Liz Freer (see Loughran & Berry, 2006: 71–4) describes her experience in implementing this procedure in her science class. Freer initially experienced this teaching procedure as a learner herself in the Science Teaching and Learning project (STaL: Catholic Education Office, Melbourne) and was encouraged to use it in her own classroom. Her case illustrates how valuable translation activities of this kind can be both for student and teacher learning.

Learning on the move

Starting off

We were mid-way through a Year 10 Science unit called 'On the move'. It was Term 3 and for many of the girls in the class this was their last semester of Science.

A collective groan echoed around the room at the mention of calculators—the idea that maths would be integrated into the Science unit created much angst for the majority of the class. Then it happened—I knew it would—the same old question came up yet again:

'Which VCE [HSC] subject is this topic related to?'

Followed by the typical response:

'I'm not doing Physics next year—it's too hard.'

In traditional fashion, I had taught the concepts of displacement, average speed, velocity and acceleration. I felt that the majority of the girls were now reasonably confident performing the basic calculations required but just how much deeper understanding was going on in their heads was debatable. Ticker timers had been introduced as a means of investigating motion. The obligatory worksheet had been completed— beautiful cut-and-paste strips of tape that formed a distance/time graph followed by a 'complete the gap' summary. Watching each group complete this task revealed that usually one person in the group provided the answers while the others listened and copied!

I reminded myself that we, as a Science faculty, were trying to encourage our students' thinking skills and the ability to work cooperatively to problem solve.

'Cut-and-paste of paper strips, or "busy work"; great for the last lesson on Friday but not really encouraging any deep-level thinking!' I thought. 'Time for a different approach,' I told myself.

Period 1, mid-week

I drew a velocity/time graph on the board [see Figure 7.6] and presented each group with a trolley.

'Are we using the ticker timers again?' chorused the class. After waiting for everyone to settle I provided instructions.

'Each group is to use the trolley to model the motion represented by the graph on the board. This demonstration is to be done for me before the group can move on to the next activity.'

Figure 7.6 Velocity/time graph 1

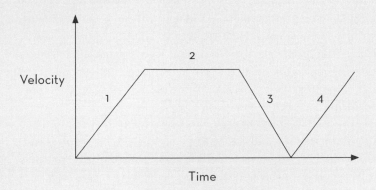

This was met with the predictable question from Susan, who requires constant reassurance during any task:

'Will you help us?'

My response to this type of question is always 'of course'. But today, I wanted each student to think for themselves and draw on the group to help problem solve. Unpredictably, I responded:

'No, your group members will assist you.'

This caused some consternation for Susan, who relied on having her progress monitored every step of the way.

In the previous lesson we had discussed the forces operating on a moving object, progressing to Newton's first law of motion:

'When role-playing the motion, each group is to explain the forces acting on the trolley at each section of the graph.'

I thought this should be possible if they got the idea last lesson. Much animated discussion followed. Susan immediately reacted:

'Miss, this is too hard, I need your help.'

Assistance was politely refused. Susan realised that help was not forthcoming and rejoined her group.

As the group worked on their role-play, Susan progressively became a more active participant within the group. Her contributions revealed an understanding of the principles behind the graph. When this group was ready to perform their role-play, Susan was a vocal, confident contributor.

I was expecting some students to suggest that section 3 on the graph represented reverse motion. I overheard Annie make this suggestion but was very pleased that her fellow students were able to explain that the motion involved deceleration, not reversing. I was pleasantly surprised that she was the only student to communicate this misunderstanding. Within the next half-hour, each group confidently demonstrated the motion of the trolley. With a little prompting, they were also able to articulate the net forces acting on the trolley but did find this to be the more difficult part of the task. It did, however, provide a springboard for future discussion.

Every student was engaged and involved during this session. Those who found it challenging to think through the problem were encouraged to brainstorm with the group instead of automatically seeking help. From my perspective, I found it reasonably simple to move between groups to listen to proceedings. Time management is always a daunting issue associated with this type of activity—that feeling of dread that descends over every brain cell as chaos fills the imagination—every group requiring your immediate attention when they all finish at the same time. Relief! Each group arrived at their solution at different times, hence watching the role-plays did not involve too much down-time or time for mischief.

Follow-up
Three lessons later, I presented the students with a slightly different graph [see Figure 7.7].

Figure 7.7 Velocity/time graph 2

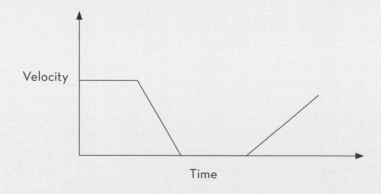

Source: adapted from Loughran & Berry, 2006: 71–4

Discussion of the motion as a group was followed by a class activity. The girls instructed our driver, Sarah, how to move the trolley from a starting point (metre ruler) on the floor. With great confidence and displaying trust in each other, the girls articulated the navigation instructions for Sarah. Nicole then demonstrated higher-order thinking skills by suggesting that the trolley could not accelerate instantly to constant speed. With agreement, the class instructed Sarah to start the trolley before the start line. They were all engaged in their learning, having an enjoyable time, and I could see that this was doing much more for their understanding about motion graphs than the busy work of the past.

I asked them what they thought about the activities.

'It was a different sort of science. I liked it. I didn't find it as difficult as nerves and things.'

'I thought that the graphs on the board were good because we were to work in groups and didn't get the teacher's help, which meant that we had to work it out ourselves.'

'I thought it was good because we could get a visual idea of how the forces and motion actually worked. It gave me a better understanding of how to relate it back to the graphs.'

'Great interaction and discussion with groups.'

'Although it was hard, working it out as a group is better.'

'It was a good activity to learn how to figure out things by ourselves.'

'It was different, much more interesting.'

In conclusion

I found it interesting that a response to this topic was that it was easier than 'nerves and things', as girls in particular usually find biology concepts more straightforward than physics. The development of problem-solving skills was an aim of this activity and their comments suggested to me that they were doing that. There is a lot of talk in schools about catering for individual differences, but it is not always easy to see how to do that in a class. This approach, however, really did cater for different learning styles, and was appreciated by students. Finally, an emphasis on group work and verbal interaction was important for many of these students. It seemed to make quite a difference in the way they stayed on task and engaged in their learning. The same applied to me too.

Overview

This chapter offered an overview of the notion of translation and situated it within the language and practice of teaching and learning. It has demonstrated how translation activities help learners to develop their understanding, especially when performed as a conscious act. As a more specialised form of processing, translation is an important component of the language of teaching and learning that supports pedagogical development.

8
Synthesising

Synthesis is the process of putting all the parts of something together to make up a coherent whole. As the previous chapters have made clear, there are a number of elements that influence learning. No single element of learning is sufficient for understanding. Rather, there is a need for learners to continually build and refine their knowledge, skills, feelings and attitudes in ways that might help to broaden what it is they know about a topic and how to use that knowledge in different situations. Synthesising is a way to create a coherent whole at a particular point in time.

Synthesising is an important method of bringing the pieces of a topic together and joining them in learning so that each of the elements interacts in such a way as to build on one another. In so doing, richer understandings of the particular content can be developed. As synthesising is a building-up process, it requires the learner to be actively engaged in considering not only the aspects of the content that might need to be assembled but also the way in which those aspects might best be combined to enhance understanding. Through the process of synthesising, questions, issues and concerns can be tapped into from a personal perspective in ways that encourage learners to pursue what they feel is important in building their knowledge. Because of this, there is a greater likelihood that individuals will begin to recognise and acknowledge that which they need to know better, and so begin to address gaps in their understanding in order to create a more coherent and holistic view of the subject under consideration.

In order to bring different elements together to create a big-picture view of particular content, there is a need for the learner to apply thinking skills such as reasoning, analysing and summarising in order to make sense of the individual elements of the content and to consider how they might fit together meaningfully. Therefore, reconsidering the nature of the elements can encourage learners to begin to search for and recognise patterns, and to create new perspectives on what once may have been taken for granted.

Another important point about synthesising is that, in bringing different parts together, the learner is creating something new. Synthesising is not about regurgitating information and ideas in an unthinking and unconnected way; it is about creating something new and extending knowledge. The central point is that the new knowledge further develops the learner's understanding. Thus, synthesising is clearly a very active process.

Understanding synthesising in the way described above is important because the process itself can sometimes be confused with summarising or paraphrasing, which are different processes with different purposes. A major point of difference between summarising, paraphrasing and synthesising is about the need to be working towards creating something new, not simply recasting the bits in a more concise form. That is not to suggest that summarising and paraphrasing are not important tools for learning. Rather, they should be seen as helpful ways of identifying and refining some of the elements to be assembled, which can then help to make the creative process of synthesising more meaningful.

Benjamin Bloom (1956) described synthesis as a higher-order thinking skill requiring the learner to be able to do such things as make informed predictions, hypothesise, invent, design, develop, and construct in ways that might lead to new and creative outcomes. Again, the notion of synthesis as an active intellectual process stands out as important for building learning strategies that move beyond the constituent parts alone to comprise a number of thinking skills, which when developed and refined make a difference for quality in learning. Predicting is one skill worth considering in more detail.

Predicting

Questioning what we know and how we know it is often initiated when we weigh up the facts about a given situation and make a prediction about the likely cause and effect and/or possible outcomes. By considering the elements of information that we think may influence what might happen in a given situation, we begin to test how well that knowledge works in a new situation. Therefore, predicting is an element of thinking that can be a stepping stone to synthesising.

Some of our thinking processes involve looking for patterns. As we encounter different events we begin to look for particular characteristics that might be common in an episode or event so that it can help to inform us about similar situations in the future. Predicting is a thinking skill that is developed and refined, sometimes subconsciously, as a result of scanning through the collection of patterns with which we are familiar and have built up over time. This is particularly evident when using intellectual strategies/algorithms (White, 1988) that we apply in an almost unthinking manner; for example, finding a book in a library. However, there are times when our familiarity with a pattern can create a false sense of security and so our predictions lead to unexpected outcomes.

Consider further what it takes to find a book in a library. Perhaps it seems a simple task, especially if it has been done a number of times before, due to familiarity with the pattern and an ability to apply the algorithm. After looking up the reference number in the catalogue, it is perhaps not so difficult to apply the cataloguing rules and find the way to the appropriate shelf and retrieve the book. If that skill is refined, it can be possible to become proficient at applying the algorithm in such a way as to predict where the book might be on the shelf by knowing what books it will be near and how the reference number is assigned, so that even without the catalogue it could be possible to home in on the book. However, if the cataloguing system is different from that with which we are familiar (for example, the US Library of Congress system as opposed to the Dewey Decimal system) then our ability to find the book, much less predict where it might be on the shelves, becomes a more challenging task. Because the system is different, applying the algorithm doesn't work. As a consequence, it takes time to actively process the information about how the new cataloguing system works before being able to recognise the patterns in the system and search for books with more confidence. With greater confidence, the ability to make more accurate predictions using the new system begins to emerge, and in time can become routine.

Making predictions is one way of initiating careful thought about the information at hand in order to make informed choices about the likely outcomes of particular events. We may very well take for granted our ability to make accurate predictions when what we think will happen does happen, but that can quickly change when challenged in new ways by predictions that do not line up with the outcomes we anticipated. It is in these times that analysis of the data, thinking through the possibilities and looking at what we already know with a more critical eye begin to really stand out in our thinking. Therefore, if we can create pedagogical episodes that require students to use thinking skills such as predicting, it is more likely that synthesising will be encouraged and so the quality of learning might be enhanced.

Recognition of the value of developing pedagogical episodes that encourage students to synthesise information, ideas, knowledge, feelings and concerns is important and can be initiated through teaching and learning activities that draw on some of the thinking skills that form the basis of synthesising (for example, categorising, combining, compiling, devising, designing, predicting, hypothesising, revising and organising). The following teaching procedures illustrate ways in which synthesising can be encouraged.

Teaching procedures: Synthesising

The Suchman technique

The Suchman technique is a good teaching procedure for getting students to think carefully and to analyse a situation before constructing hypotheses to test their explanations. It works well when attempting to explore and explain curious/puzzling situations. The technique works in the following way:

1 The teacher presents students with a curious or puzzling situation (the explanation of the situation should be discoverable—it is not meant to be a trick).

2 Students then ask the teacher questions to gather data. The questions must be closed questions—with yes/no answers only. If not, they need to rephrase their question. The questions should be worded in such a way that the answer could be determined from observation alone.

3 Students consider what they have learnt from their questions and attempt to explain the situation and suggest possible solutions; that is, hypothesise. The teacher should ensure that the number of hypotheses is not too great as they need to see how the different hypotheses relate to their data. This process continues until the situation has been resolved and the students have solved the puzzle.

4 Together the class reflect on and analyse the process they have just been involved in. For example, students may ask: What questions worked best? What information was of most/least help? How did we arrive at the solution? What other issues/ ideas do we now have?

An important aspect of the Suchman technique is in helping students learn to distinguish between fact-finding questions and those that examine the relationships between variables in the puzzle situation. The Suchman technique has also been found to help students listen more carefully to each other and the teacher. The following (edited) example is taken from a discussion following a class viewing of the movie *The Elephant Man* and illustrates the technique in action. In this case, students would need to have a basic familiarity with the concepts of DNA, chromosomes and genes.

The Elephant Man

Student: Is it a disease?
Teacher: Yes.
Student: Was it caused by something he ate?
Teacher: No.
Student: Is it caused by a virus?

Teacher:	No.
Student:	Is it caused by bacteria?
Teacher:	No.
Student:	Would he have been born with the disease?
Teacher:	Yes.
Student:	Did the Elephant Man's mother or father have these abnormalities?
Teacher:	No.
Student:	Did his brothers or sisters have the disease?
Teacher:	No.
Student:	Is it an inherited disease?
Teacher:	Yes, it is. (This may lead to many questions about dominant and recessive genes and inheritance of disease, but the answers may not match the students' understanding of inheritance.)
Student:	Is his the only case of this disease?
Teacher:	No.
Student:	Did his mother get a disease when she was pregnant, like German measles?
Teacher:	Perhaps—it is possible.
Student:	If she did get a disease is it possible that it might have caused one of her genes or one of her baby's genes to change in some way?
Teacher:	Yes—it is possible.

From asking questions using the Suchman technique, the students are on the path to discovering for themselves the possibility of spontaneous changes in genetic material. (Source: Grant, Johnson & Sanders, 1990: 23–4)

What can you work out?

This teaching procedure is organised around the idea of offering students a limited amount of information (in the example in Figure 8.1 it is a map and a small piece of text) from which they then attempt to work out as much as they can about the situation, and any prior knowledge about the subject, and to write questions for anything they need to know more about.

Figure 8.1 What can you work out?: Terra Australis

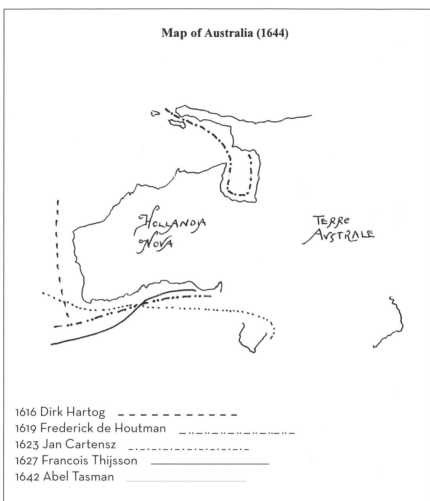

Map of Australia (1644)

1616 Dirk Hartog – – – – – – – – – –
1619 Frederick de Houtman   – ·· – ·· – ·· – ·· – ·· – ··
1623 Jan Cartensz   – · – · – · – · – · – · –
1627 Francois Thijsson   ————————
1642 Abel Tasman   ···························

In 1768 James Cook left England for the Pacific Ocean to observe the transit of Venus from Tahiti. He sailed westerly via Cape Horn, arriving there in 1769. On the trip home he explored the South Pacific looking for 'Terra Australis'. He first reached New Zealand, and then sailed further west to the south-east corner of Australia in 1770. From there he sailed north along the east coast through to the Torres Strait and on to Batavia, Dutch East Indies, and back to England via the Indian Ocean and the Cape of Good Hope.

Jigsaw groupwork method

The jigsaw groupwork method is based around the formation of two groupings of students. The first is the Home Group and the second is the Expert Group. The number of students in a group is dependent on the number of questions to be completed (for example, four questions for four members in a group). In the Home Group students decide on the question that each will answer—a different question for each student. Students then leave their Home Group and form Expert Groups with all the other students from the other Home Groups who selected the same question.

In the Expert Group, students come to a consensus about the answer that they will take back to their Home Group. It is important that all members of the Expert Group understand the answer as fully as possible because when they return to their Home Group they will be responsible for teaching their group about that question topic. In their Home Group they will be the Expert, the person who teaches the rest of the group and responds to any questions, issues or concerns.

This teaching procedure works well because of two important aspects of learning. The first is related to the fact that students work together in the Expert Group to share ideas and arrive at a consensus about what to present to their Home Group. The second is in the learning that occurs when students assume the role of teacher and think carefully about how and what they are going to present.

Before–Now–After

This is a teaching procedure that works well, especially when using visual stimulus. Students are shown a photograph, small piece of text or film clip (representing 'Now') and are then asked to hypothesise or think about what led to the situation (Before) and to predict what might happen following the situation (After).

Before before/after after

This is another example of how a teaching procedure can be developed and refined. Jo Osler and Jill Flack (2008) adapted and adjusted the Before–Now–After procedure (see Figure 8.2) and used it extensively with their primary school students. Through their documenting of this procedure other teachers have used it and have reported that it works equally well with secondary school students.

In this activity, students are asked to brainstorm what they can see in the visual stimulus material and think about what might have happened before the situation, and then what might have happened *before* the before. Similarly, they are also asked to think about what might have happened after the situation, and then *after* the after.

Figure 8.2 Before before, after after

An interesting aspect of this teaching procedure is associated with the timeframe allocated to the befores and afters. For example, consider the variations possible and the different types of thinking that might arise as the timeframe varies from hours to days, weeks, years, and so on.

Postbox

For this procedure the teacher constructs a series of numbered questions/prompts on the topic being studied. The questions/prompts should be structured in such a way as to draw on a diversity of opinions from members of the class (that is, not closed questions with a definitive answer). Students individually write their responses to the questions on separate sheets of paper. They then post their responses corresponding to the question numbers into numbered boxes.

The class is then divided into groups and each group accepts responsibility for one of the postboxes. The group reads the responses and attempts to categorise them. They then prepare a presentation to illustrate the range of views about the question/prompt to the rest of the class.

An extension of this activity is for groups to then set a task based on the data they have been working with and to present that to another group to complete.

Learning from discussion

It has been well reported that students can easily overlook the value of discussion because they do not necessarily link dialogue with learning. Therefore, although they may well enjoy a class discussion, there is always the possibility that at the end of the discussion they do very little to actively consolidate their learning.

Learning from discussion is a structured way of demonstrating to students not only what they have learnt, but also how they have learnt through discussion. This teaching procedure requires students to keep a running list of the issues raised during a discussion and then to analyse that data and formulate their own personal conclusion. They might also be asked to make a list of any questions, issues or concerns that have not been addressed in the discussion that they feel are important in terms of reaching a satisfactory conclusion.

As students become more adept at being involved in class discussion and analysing and questioning themselves as they go along, they become more conscious of their thinking and can become more informed about what they know and what they need to know more about.

Design and create a learning artefact

A challenging end-of-unit synthesising activity is to ask students to design and create their own representation of their learning (for example, a poster) and to then present and defend it in small groups or to the class. This activity works best if it is genuinely open-ended and students are encouraged to be as imaginative and creative as possible as they explore what they have learnt and what they think they need to learn more about and how that might be represented to others.

Fishbowl discussion

This teaching procedure involves conducting a planned discussion at an appropriate time during a unit of work when the teacher feels as though the students have enough knowledge of the topic to be involved in a thoughtful discussion. The procedure works as follows:

1 The teacher writes two questions on the board (questions A and B).

2 Students form pairs and each pair brainstorms possible answers to both questions.

3 Members of each pair choose one of the questions, A or B. All A members will be discussing possible answers to question A, while all B members will be discussing question B. Discussion of each question will take place separately.

4 All A members form a seated circle while all B members form a circle around the outside of the A members' circle—usually standing behind their A partner in such a way that B members can observe the discussion taking place.

5 In a fishbowl discussion those in the outer circle observe those in the inner circle as they discuss their responses to the question. Outer circle members observe the discussion and at the end comment on how it went.

6 Once discussion on question A is complete, the members swap positions.

A good fishbowl discussion occurs when students listen to, and build on, what was said before, speak a limited number of times (by adding their view or asking a question when it is most appropriate) and question ideas, not people.

Structured thinking

This teaching procedure was developed by a group of PEEL teachers after their students pointed out that when they (the teachers) were working on a problem, they used some higher-order thinking that extended beyond what the students could do. As a consequence this led some of these teachers to reflect on how they tackled tasks and to develop a set of steps to show their thinking to their students as a guide for how they might do something similar. Central to this teaching procedure is that the instructions are not meant to be followed in a recipe style. Rather, they are designed to illustrate how experts structure their thinking when addressing a problem. The following example demonstrates structured thinking on how to read a poem.

How to read a poem

Students were asked to write notes on the questions below. They were told to write whatever they felt or thought, and not be concerned about the 'right' answer. They then read the poem through to the end twice.

- Why do you think the poem has the title it has? Give some possible reasons.
- What puzzles you?
- Do you know the meanings of words? Look up any you don't know in the dictionary.
- Do you know the meanings of expressions or groups of words? Guess some possible meanings.
- Make up some questions beginning with 'why' and 'how'.
- Make up some possible answers to these questions.
- What connections are there between the poem and its title?
- Is there any imagery? Note similes, metaphors and personification. Are there any connections between these and the title?
- Is there any rhyme or rhythm? Note any uses of alliteration, assonance, internal rhyme, long and short vowel sounds, repetition and rhyme patterns. Are there any connections between these and the title?
- Pick out what you think are the key words or expressions. Are there any connections between these and the title?
- Look at the lengths of the lines and the number of lines in each verse. Is there anything usual? Is there a reason for the way the poem is set out? Is there any link with the meaning?
- Can you find any contrasts or opposites in the poem, either in images, sounds, setting out or meanings? Is there any link with the overall meaning?

> - What is a possible meaning for the whole poem? Does the title make any more sense to you? (adapted from Baird & Northfield, 1992: 256-7)

Continuum

This teaching procedure is organised around using the key words or concepts in a multi-linked process (similar to a flow diagram). Students individually (or in pairs, depending on how many words there are that make up the process) are given a key word. They then think carefully about where the word goes in the continuum and physically place the word in the appropriate space when called on to do so. They must also justify why they think their word should be at that particular point.

In a compelling study into her own classroom teaching, Lynn Boyle discussed how she used a continuum based on a river system with her Year 7 Studies of Society and the Environment (SOSE) class. Interestingly, she makes it clear how it was just as important for her to become familiar with using this teaching procedure as it was for her students. In fact, the first time she used the continuum it was a disaster. However, she knew it should have worked better and so decided to try it a second time and, as the edited extract below demonstrates, it led to much better learning outcomes.

Experiencing the continuum

It's the last period on Thursday. I'm behind in the curriculum with my Year 7 SOSE class. I have to find a way to moderate their need to have so many questions answered, to engage them ... and GET ON WITH THE COURSE! They file in—rowdy after their last class but I'm not deterred. We have an activity to finish before we get on to the task I WANT to do this lesson.

We've been undertaking a study of 'the Earth', but every topic we've discussed has taken twice as long as I anticipated. Their questions, dare I say, are driving me nuts, but I don't admit that to anyone—after all, questioning is what we want! I put an end to their never-ending questions about rivers by telling them we don't have time for any more questions right now; we have an activity we must complete this lesson.

We've talked about rivers, answered a million questions about rivers and completed the comprehension questions from their compulsory text. I want to try the river continuum—it's a hands-on activity. I'm tired of all the text-based work. I want the class to have fun with their learning.

I demand their attention.

'Listen carefully,' I say. 'I'm going to give everyone a card. On the card you will find a word which has something to do with a river system. Then we're all going to stand up and make a circle around the tables I've carefully arranged down the centre of the room. When I say! NOT NOW! When I tell you!'

I look to my folder for my cards—they've disappeared. I search frantically—more time wasted. They're nowhere to be found. I throw a sheet of blank paper at each student as I rush around the room.

'I'm going to tell you what word to write as I come around, so listen carefully!' I splutter.

I hear, from the far corner, the questions starting again:

'How do you spell DELTA?'

'I've got that word—why are you giving it to Simon?'

'How big does the writing have to be?'

'Can I use texta?'

I'm oblivious to all the questions. At last we have some sort of order and everyone has a card with a word related to rivers written on it—I hope that everyone can understand what the cards say—the spelling is atrocious.

Several hours later, or so it seems, the students are lined up around the tables.

I start speaking. 'Okay, this is how it works. We're going to start with Andrea. She's going to place her card on the table where she thinks it should go in a real river system; at the start, the end, or somewhere in the middle. Joanne will go next (she's a bright girl so I know she'll do this well, I think to myself) and then we'll follow in order around the room. When Joanne puts her card down she has to explain why she's put it there, why her part of the river system should go there. Everyone has to do the same. You can change the order of any card when it comes to your turn but you must justify the move.'

At the end of the tables a few boys are pushing each other, another boy has sat down and the girls down the back are squirming restlessly. Joanne places her 'meander' card with a brilliant explanation. Mathew is next. He wants to pass. 'NO PASSING,' I say. He places the card on the table with no justification other than, 'That's where I want to put it'. This sets the scene for several others. A few of the students think carefully about where their cards should go and justify their choices admirably, but the majority of students are chatting to one another and moving as far away from the central tables as possible. We get almost to the last student when the bell rings. I believe I hear a sigh as students rush back to the safety of their own tables and begin to pack up.

What a disaster! I can't wait to get out of the room, out of the school. I don't ever want to see a continuum activity again. I leave the classroom thankful that this disaster is over. The sigh of relief now is my own. Tomorrow we can start something new and I won't ever have to think about this failure again. To add to my pain I arrive back to my desk to find the brightly coloured, laminated, correctly spelled river systems cards in a neat pile. I talk to no one and get out of my staff room as fast as I can, defeated and deflated.

As I drive home I start to cool off—it's a long drive. I can't help but reflect on the session and my own questioning process begins. It IS a good procedure! Why didn't it work? By dinner I have a list of at least ten possible reasons.

I have the class first period the next morning and I start by telling them that I'd really like to do the continuum activity again. I think I detect groans from the back of the room but I swallow my pride and move on. I explain why I want to give it another go: 'It's a great way for you to check your own understanding of river systems and especially to learn to justify your opinions.'

A hand shoots up, 'What does justify mean?'

We work out the meaning and I ask for further questions before we start.

'What's a billabong?'

'What's a riffle?'

'I'm not sure when the meander is eroded and when it deposits.'

'What does deposit mean?'

We run through all the terms in the continuum and I jot key

words and meanings on the board for reference. Finally the class agrees that we will give the continuum another go.

We take our cards and sit in a circle on the floor at the back of the room. Everyone is looking pretty comfortable and relaxed. We establish some rules on talking during others' turn and clarify you can move any of the cards when it's your turn but you have to explain why you are doing it. You mustn't interrupt another person but you can have another turn second time around. I ask who would like to start. Surprisingly, several hands go up. The process begins slowly but students are aware of how the procedure should work and what their cards mean (the definitions are still on the board so they can refer to them if needed). We get to student six or seven and I detect some squirming again.

To my delight I realise that it's not discomfort or lack of interest that's creating this movement. I see hands over several mouths as I realise that students are stopping themselves from interrupting other students' justifications. The squirming is now through enthusiasm and an eagerness to have another turn, or to change the order of the continuum. Students who rarely contribute in class are eager and even confident when it is their turn. Some place only their own card but many challenge other students' opinions and move the continuum through their own justifications.

We're again close to finishing when the bell rings. Only four students stand up to leave! The eager eyes of each student are on their own card and where it's been moved to. Several students cannot contain themselves and take the bell as an opportunity to have their say. An argument ensues over the 'correct' order of the continuum. I placate further dispute by explaining that several orders can be correct and that it is the process of justification that is important. I congratulate the class on their best lesson of the year. They give themselves a rowdy round of applause and reluctantly leave for their next class. (Boyle, 2002: 81–4)

Overview

This chapter provided a summary of the ideas surrounding synthesising and how it can be used within the language and practice of teaching and learning. It has highlighted the importance for learners to continually build and refine their knowledge. Syntheses help to build richer understandings of the particular content under consideration and encourage the learner to approach building up their learning from a personal perspective. As a part of the language of teaching and learning, synthesising stands out as a way of encouraging a pedagogical intent focused on developing a coherent and holistic view of subject matter.

9
Metacognition

The previous chapters have largely focused attention on cognition —the mental processes used to code, store, transform and retrieve information, ideas and knowledge. Metacognition operates at a different level and has been described as thinking about thinking (Flavell, 1976). Metacognition helps us to know or decide which mental process(es) to use in a given situation, at a given time and for a particular reason—hence the tag of thinking about thinking. We are all metacognitive. However, the level of metacognition employed or, put another way, the range of metacognitive skills we have and use, varies from individual to individual and from context to context.

Encouraging learners to enhance their metacognitive skills offers real possibilities for changing the rhetoric of active, responsible learners in classrooms because metacognition involves self-monitoring and self-regulation. When self-regulated learners are faced with a task, they typically tend to:

- analyse the task and interpret task requirements;
- set task-specific goals that aid successful task completion;
- self-monitor progress and provide 'self-feedback';
- adjust strategies and goals throughout the process; and
- use self-motivational strategies to ensure task completion.

Metacognition thus involves planning, monitoring, regulating, questioning, reflecting on and reviewing our cognitive processes. (Krause et al., 2003: 145)

It is not difficult to see, then, how metacognition can make a differ-ence in learning and in unlocking new avenues to teaching for high quality learning.

There are many types of metacognitive skills and strategies but at the broadest level three main strategies are most commonly noted in the literature: *planning*, *monitoring*, and *evaluating*. A typically successful school learner would most likely employ strategies from each of these categories in order to successfully complete a set task. For example, in planning for the task at hand, metacognitive students are likely to ask themselves questions such as: What is the purpose of the task? What do I need to do to complete the task? What do I want to achieve from the task? How much time and energy should I devote to the task? Similarly, once involved in the task, a degree of monitoring helps to align what is happening with what was planned. Monitor-ing questions might include such things as: How do I feel this task is going? Am I making sufficient progress? Are there any changes I need to make to what I am doing? Am I meeting my goals? At the completion of the task, evaluation questions might include: How well did I complete the task? What did I do well? What could I have done better? What would I do differently if I was doing it again?

One way of interpreting the actions of students who think about their thinking in the way described above is that they are asking of themselves the types of questions that we as teachers often ask our students to help them successfully complete their set work. This then raises an interesting point about what it means to learn to be more metacognitive; it requires a conscious effort. Therefore, to develop and enhance students' metacognition there is a need to explicitly link that skill development to the way we teach, which means that the teaching procedures we use should challenge students' thinking—and their thinking about thinking. PEEL (Project for Enhancing Effective Learning, Baird & Mitchell, 1986; Baird & Northfield, 1992) grew out of teachers' desire to do just that.

PEEL: Teaching for metacognition

In an extended study of classroom teaching and learning John Baird (1986a) found out a great deal about how students do *not* learn. His study was ground-breaking at the time because it shifted the focus

of attention from the teacher to the learner. He described five asser-
tions that encapsulated the essence of his observations of students'
classroom learning:

1 Learning outcomes are determined by decisions made by the
   learner.

2 Inadequate learning is due to inadequate decision-making.

3 Learners are often unaware of their learning problems. This
   lack of awareness generates poor attitudes.

4 It takes energy to learn with understanding, or to unlearn a
   misconception.

5 Increasing awareness of the nature and process of learning
   leads to improved attitudes and procedures.

Under his second assertion (on inadequate learning) Baird outlined
seven habits that were later described as poor learning tendencies
(for a full explanation see Baird, 1986b), which he saw as being at the
core of students' 'unknowing' approach to learning. These included:
impulsive attention; superficial attention; inappropriate application;
inadequate monitoring; premature closure; ineffective restructuring;
and lack of reflective thinking.

We can all identify with these poor learning tendencies for it
is not just our students who display them. For example, superficial
attention is something we regularly experience—it could be happening to you now. When reading something, you may be briefly
distracted. Upon returning to the text you may find that you inadvertently reread the same text that you were reading before the
interruption—sometimes this happens more than once—and find it
difficult to know what place you were up to in the text. This is an
example of superficial attention—scanning the information without
sufficient processing. Of course, in some instances this can also be
a useful strategy for dealing with large amounts of text. The issue
though is the difference between knowingly and unknowingly acting in a particular way.

As Baird explained, these poor learning tendencies are 'related
to bad processing habits during learning. [They are] symptoms of a
lack of informed, active involvement in the learning process [and

cause] learners to make inappropriate decisions about their learning; these decisions militate against successful performance' (Baird, 1986b: 7). Not surprisingly, he noted that more successful learners displayed fewer of these poor learning tendencies than less successful learners.

Baird's study tapped into what many teachers recognise as passive learning but, importantly, he offered some useful labels and descriptions (poor learning tendencies) that invited teachers to think about ways of addressing passive learning as identifiable targets rather than as an amorphous whole. In so doing, teachers were also encouraged to look at their teaching differently and to share their efforts in organised and thoughtful ways. One such teacher was Ian Mitchell, and through Baird's theoretical perspective and Mitchell's teaching position, theory and practice fused and PEEL was established.

In many ways, then, PEEL teachers were at the forefront of the groundswell of later changes in ideas and approaches to teaching and learning in schools, generically described as the teaching of thinking skills. However, the work of PEEL teachers had a subtly different edge because it was purposely directed towards encouraging students to be aware of their own learning and for teachers to accept that they actually had a major ongoing role in ensuring that that would happen. From that perspective, teaching could not be viewed as a one-way process (that is, delivery only) and learning had to be understood as much more than receiving.

PEEL grew into an organised and focused project that had, as one outcome among many others, the building up and documenting of teaching procedures purposely designed to encourage students to be more metacognitive. The key to challenging students' approaches to learning was cleverly crafted by PEEL teachers through conceptualising teaching as something that needed to act on poor learning tendencies not as a negative (that is, trying to find and fix a problem), but as a positive (supporting and encouraging good learning habits). So they developed what came to be known as *good learning behaviours* (GLBs—for a full description and explanation see Chapter 4 of Baird & Northfield, 1992). For example, some GLBs include students telling the teacher when they do not understand; planning a general strategy before starting work;

seeking links between different subjects; expressing disagreement; justifying opinions; or (appropriately) challenging the text or an answer that the teacher sanctions as correct. Clearly, encouraging the development of GLBs requires a supportive teaching and learning environment, as the honest and genuine sharing at the heart of such pedagogy requires well-nurtured trust—something built over time through a teacher's practice.

Even though PEEL was initiated in the mid 1980s, the core purpose of enhancing student learning through a focus on metacognition continues to ring true as a major goal for practice and, in so doing, helps to focus the educational spotlight on to the notion of pedagogy, as opposed to teaching and learning as separate and discrete entities. The purpose of PEEL was to teach for enhanced metacognition—that is, not something just done once after which all the problems of student learning were solved. Teaching for metacognition is something that needs to be worked at over and over again, reinforced through practice and continually developed and refined.

Over the years the notion of teaching for enhanced metacognition has been taken up in many ways. However, at the heart of this work is a paradox that can sometimes be misleading to even the most informed and thoughtful teacher. It has been demonstrated time and time again that despite our best intentions and efforts to teach in ways that encourage active student learning, research suggests that for many of us our purpose and our practice are not always so perfectly aligned. The difficulty is that in the bustling world of teaching it is not always easy to really see our own practice, much less see it from other perspectives. Therefore, sometimes we need to be challenged and confronted by our own teaching—just like students need to be challenged and confronted by their learning. This point was very well made by Damien Hynes, who was confronted by his perception of his teaching through his students' learning. In the extract below, Hynes illustrates the essence of the paradox noted above and demonstrates how important it is for us to continually strive to better align purpose with practice.

The turning point

After encouraging students to ask questions, think about what they are doing, show initiative, etc. and getting passive or negative results, I wrote notes on the board which students mechanically copied down. I held a geography book in my hand and pretended to copy the two paragraphs shown below from the text.

Water
The degree of rainfall for each half year and the annual seasonal deficit are the systems which determine which areas will receive rain and which won't. However, in planning where to plant crops it is not enough to know the system, one must also take account of the different levels within each seasonal system. We must also know how much of the soil will be lost by evaporation.

Length of daylight period
Plants depend on light. The daylight hours vary from town to town depending on altitude. Towns in low lying areas depend largely on the degree of photosynthesis and rainfall—clouds create shade which affects people's vision. The plant's visionary cycle and light condensation greatly affect the amount of hygration that can exist in a certain town at a certain time. Melbourne's hygration can vary by 20 cm from Sydney's at any particular time.

This procedure was a spur of the moment decision. I made the nonsense notes up on the spot . . . I waited until all students had copied the notes and then asked if anyone had any questions. I asked this a number of times, and to my recollection, out of two Year 10 classes only one student per class had a question. One asked the meaning of a term used, the other hesitantly questioned whether soil could evaporate. I guess it was from this point on that I realised three things.

Firstly, I thought I had been teaching in a fashion that encouraged student involvement and initiative. I now realised that I had not been challenging the students enough. My reaction to these two classes was one of concern about my teaching methods.

Secondly, I was surprised to see to what extent students expect teachers to dictate and dominate class situations. Students either believe that teachers should not be questioned or believe it is much easier not to get involved in class discussion.

Thirdly, I realised that as a teacher I had an obligation to alter my teaching strategies. Even though I believed that I was using strategies that the PEEL project professed, I had to have a much closer look at the project and adapt it to my classroom methods. (Hynes, 1986: 22-3)

Hynes was a conscientious, hard-working, diligent professional who was seriously concerned about his students' learning. However, as we have all experienced, daily demands of teaching can work on us (just as it works on students) to transform practice into routines and scripts that, sadly, can diminish our good intentions and unknowingly trigger passive learning responses in our students. This is an issue that those outside of teaching think can be easily resolved—usually by some top-down policy mandate—but those whose work is based in classrooms, the crucible of teaching and learning, recognise this situation as the ongoing challenge of teaching, something that the expert pedagogue manages in idiosyncratic and professional ways. The situation is not something easily able to be fixed by applying a recipe or formula; rather, the manner of the response is in fact a demonstration of the wisdom of practice which forms the foundations of teachers' professional knowledge.

Teaching for enhanced metacognition has been developed and refined over the years because teachers have moved beyond teaching as a series of activities to seriously explore teaching and learning as a relationship. This has led some to see into pedagogy in new ways. One very strong example of this is in the work of Jo Osler and Jill Flack (see their book, *Whose learning is it? Developing children as active and responsible learners*, 2008), two teachers who documented and demonstrated how they taught their students to accept greater responsibility for their own learning.

Osler and Flack developed a deep appreciation of pedagogy because they shared their learning about teaching with one another as they taught their students how to think about their learning and to be active decision-makers in the classroom. Through that process, teaching and learning came together in ways that allowed them to not only fundamentally change the way their classrooms operated, but also helped them to become experts at articulating what they were doing, as well as how and why, in ways that made their professional knowledge of practice clear, meaningful and useable by others. It is in this sharing of knowledge that real pedagogical development is able to be realised so that it moves beyond the individual and becomes the hallmark of a professional.

Teaching procedures: Metacognition

Predict–Observe–Explain (POE)

The POE process encourages metacognition through engagement in a series of linked activities. This teaching procedure works in the following way.

1 *Predict*: students are presented with a particular situation and asked to predict the likely outcome when a change is made. After committing to their predictions, the change is made to the situation.

2 *Observe*: students carefully observe the change to the situation and make a list of the things they see happen through the change.

3 *Explain*: students are asked to explain the difference between what happened and what they expected to happen. It can be as challenging for students to explain a correct prediction as it is to explain an incorrect prediction.

The POE requires the teacher to withhold judgement and to work towards an explanation of the situation through an interpretive discussion—it is not about telling students the right answer at the end; hopefully it is arrived at through the discussion.

A good POE is based on a situation or event that students feel comfortable making predictions about so that their predictions are based on their thinking, and their questioning of that thinking, as opposed to simply making a guess. After all the students have committed themselves to a particular prediction, the teacher might canvas the range of predictions to get a feel for the various ideas in the class.

Again, it is important not to accept or reject predictions but to support students in thinking carefully about the predictions they have made.

The observation phase can be very interesting because it is easy when observing to see what we predict as opposed to what really happened. Sometimes it can be very helpful to repeat the activity so that students can observe a number of times.

The explanation process relies heavily on teacher questioning and supportive and thoughtful discussion so as to encourage students to personally reconcile the differences between their predictions and the outcomes—or if they predicted correctly, to be able to explain that publicly. Helping students confront their own cognitive dissonance is a catalyst for metacognition. Making that public through interpretive discussion requires pedagogical skill and expertise.

Constructing a list of good learning behaviours

Perhaps one of the most obvious ways of drawing attention to metacognition is for students to talk about and develop their own list of good learning behaviours (GLBs).

As outlined at the beginning of this chapter, one way of approaching metacognition is by focusing students' attention on the three big-picture metacognitive strategies: determining what a task requires; monitoring progress while doing the task; and evaluating the quality of the learning on completion. By adapting these strategies, students can learn to ask themselves many questions about their learning that can help to make metacognition an explicit and central component of it. For example, students' metacognitive strategies might be displayed through some of the following:

- concentrating on the task at hand;
- completing tasks;
- reviewing assessments of work to see where they have lost marks;
- telling the teacher when they do not understand;
- disagreeing with statements by the teacher or fellow students;
- telling the teacher when they need to know more about the topic;
- checking work;

- asking the teacher where they went wrong;
- offering real life/personal examples relevant to the topic;
- asking 'why' and 'what if' questions;
- following up on issues raised in class;
- seeing links to other work;
- looking back through earlier work when 'stuck'; and
- justifying opinions.

In his extended study of his classroom teaching, Jeff Northfield (Loughran & Northfield, 1996) organised sessions with his class to discuss learning. In these sessions he created a forum for students to think about and then set the agenda for the types of things they could do to enhance their learning about learning. In constructing their own lists of GLBs, students are able to think carefully about how to approach and improve their learning.

Responding to GLBs

One variation on constructing a class list of good learning behaviours that Jeff Northfield also tried was to present his students with a short list of GLBs (see the list of nine below), from which he asked them to choose two they would like to respond to. The list he gave his class included:

1. asking the teacher when they do not understand;
2. doing extra work to make sure they can understand and do the task;
3. suggesting new ideas and thinking of other explanations;
4. asking questions about new work;
5. trying to link new ideas to other work in school and experiences at home;
6. checking all work to see that everything has been done;
7. making sure they are clear about what they have to do and why they have to do it;
8. thinking about an idea and their plans to answer before giving an answer; and
9. taking care in presenting their work and making their notes.

Through this approach Northfield not only raised his students' consciousness about metacognition (through the GLBs), but he also gleaned important insights into things that influenced his students' thinking about using GLBs. For example, in response to GLB 1, some students said that 'asking questions wasted time'; GLB 2: 'they [students] will never understand anyway'; GLB 3: 'someone else will always suggest a better idea than me . . . they will think I am silly'; and GLB 4: 'people will think I am dumb' (Loughran & Northfield, 1996: 96–7). This information made a big difference to the way Northfield approached implementing GLBs in the classroom.

L-files

Gillian Pinnis developed L-files with her Year 7 General Studies class. She recognised that many teachers establish classroom rules for good learning at the start of the school year but the way the rules were phrased—and perhaps sometimes policed—made them appear to be more about 'classroom management than active, metacognitive learning' (Pinnis, 2002: 153). She set out to develop a learning environment through a method that would:

- teach students good learning behaviours;
- make it easy to refer back to GLBs consistently throughout the year;
- be integrated into the curriculum rather than adding to it;
- be simple and straightforward so other teachers could use it;
- give students ownership of their learning and the method; and
- be fun.

Using a list of GLBs, Pinnis constructed booklets (L-files) that were small, bright yellow and cute so that they would be attractive to students. Each had a small car on the cover. Students were made responsible for assembling their booklet, which contained one GLB per page. To use the book, students had to demonstrate each GLB. When they had done so, they could approach their teacher to sign the appropriate page. When all the pages were signed, the students would be awarded their P-plates and a small red sticker with a 'P' attached to the car on their booklet to indicate that they were a Proficient pupil.

The L-files worked exceptionally well. They were used across the whole year level, which meant students could get any of their teachers to sign off on their GLBs; it was not limited to one or two classes. The program was so successful that Pinnis conducted a research project into the influence of L-files as a tool for enhancing student's metacognition and concluded that:

> this group of students became very aware of the fact that there is a difference between passive and active learning—that certain learning behaviours would lead them to be metacognitive, to be able to think about their thinking . . . the fact that, after 12 months had elapsed, the students' use of good learning behaviours had continued was perhaps the most rewarding outcome of the study (Pinnis, 2002: 167).

Self-assessed learning: Student as teacher

Using the three broad metacognitive strategies (planning, monitoring and evaluating), it can be very helpful for students to be given an opportunity to reflect on the way they have completed a task. By referring back to planning, monitoring and evaluating, and reflecting on what they have done well and what they might have been able to do differently, students can be encouraged to think about how they have approached their learning by using these elements as tools for checking and revising before handing in their work and as ways of reviewing their work following assessment.

Another way of thinking about this procedure is in terms of the 'student as teacher'. After reviewing their work using the three broad metacognitive strategies, students choose (or are given) a topic from the unit of work and are asked to prepare a short (five-minute) presentation to teach their partner (or small group) about the topic.

List of procedures

The way that Jo Osler and Jill Flack empower their students as learners is immediately apparent in the nature of the displays and posters around their classrooms. One in particular is their list of procedures, which acts as a reminder of the variety of teaching and learning approaches used with their students.

Each time they introduce a new procedure to the class they create an icon for that procedure and attach it to the procedure list. As any visitor to the classroom can attest, their students are exceptionally comfortable with visiting the list at various stages during a unit of work in order to think about an appropriate way to approach their learning. The list is a concrete reminder to students that not all learning has to occur in the same way or through the same methods. In fact, is interesting to see young students' metacognition being made explicit and tangible through choosing to visit the list to think about the type of procedure that might be appropriate for the task at hand—very metacognitive.

Knowing what type of thinking is needed

This teaching procedure is based on Bloom's taxonomy (see Chapter 2). Students need to be familiar with each of the domains and the types of tasks that are illustrative of those domains (see Table 9.1). When that is the case, and before they embark on a task, it can be very helpful for students to consider the particular domains that apply so that they plan to appropriately cover them in the way they complete the set activity—and to review the work in the same way when it is finished.

Recounting

This is a particularly useful teaching procedure to use following an extended activity; for example, a field excursion or a camp at the end of a unit of work. Students develop a point-form list of the things that happened and what they think they learnt from those events or episodes as well as those things that they feel they did not fully understand (and would like to spend more time studying). From the point-form list, which could also be shared in pairs, small groups or through whole class discussion, students write their own review of the situation before sharing it with another student. In the sharing process, students write questions about the things they feel are not clear or that illustrate a different perspective from their own and note why. This teaching procedure then encourages students to question what they have done and how, what they have learnt and what they need to learn more about—all based on their own questioning of their learning.

Table 9.1 Action and question stems

Domain	Examples of actions	Examples of question stems
Knowledge	Telling, describing, finding, writing, naming, listing . . .	What happened when . . .? What is the meaning of . . .? Is this true or false? How much . . .?
Comprehension	Explaining, interpreting, discussing, comparing, distinguishing . . .	Can you paraphrase . . .? What is an example of . . .? What was the main idea . . .?
Application	Solving, illustrating, constructing, categorising . . .	Could this have happened in . . .? How does this apply to how you . . .? What instructions would you write for someone else to follow?
Analysis	Comparing, contrasting, analysing, investigating, categorising, explaining, identifying . . .	What was important about . . .? What was the difference between . . .? Can you compare with . . .?
Synthesis	Creating, inventing, predicting, constructing, designing, composing, formulating . . .	Can you design . . . that will . . .? Can you write a song . . .? What would happen if . . .? What solutions can you see to . . .?
Evaluation	Judging, recommending, deciding, assessing, prioritising, verifying . . .	Is there a better way of . . .? How effective is . . .? How do you feel about . . .? What would you recommend . . .?

Venn diagrams

Mathematics teachers are very familiar with Venn diagrams. However, they can be equally valuable in any other subject area. Venn diagrams are used to show the relationship between things. They work exceptionally well for exploring the depth of students' understanding of definitions and how to appropriately apply them. Venn diagrams become increasingly difficult (and therefore require much more self questioning) as the number of terms used increases. For example, the two Venn diagrams for plants and animals (Figure 9.1) explore understandings of how these two organisms might be understood in terms of classification. As they illustrate, there is a major difference between a typical student's response (separate circles) and a biologist's (small overlap), which goes to the heart of the difference in understanding biological classification. However, a Venn diagram for convicts, criminals and prisoners places different demands on the learner (try doing it yourself). Moving beyond four terms in a Venn diagram can make the task too difficult to satisfactorily complete. The choice and number of terms need to be carefully considered when using this teaching procedure.

Constructing a Venn diagram is one aspect of using this teaching procedure. The second is in the discussion that follows because, in many ways, a Venn diagram offers diagnostic advice about students' learning that can be the basis for a very valuable interpretive discussion.

Figure 9.1 Venn diagrams: Plants and animals

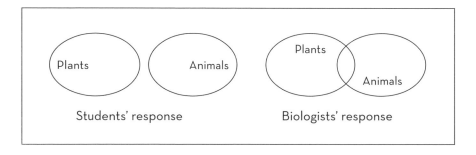

Moving-on map

Another teaching procedure developed by Jo Osler and Jill Flack is what they describe as a moving-on map (see Figure 9.2). They identified the development of their students' metacognition as a central focus of their teaching and so many of their procedures were developed by questioning their thinking about how to develop their students' metacognition. Students use the moving-on map to work out for themselves what to do when they are stuck. Osler and Flack describe the development of the moving-on map below.

Figure 9.2 Moving-on map

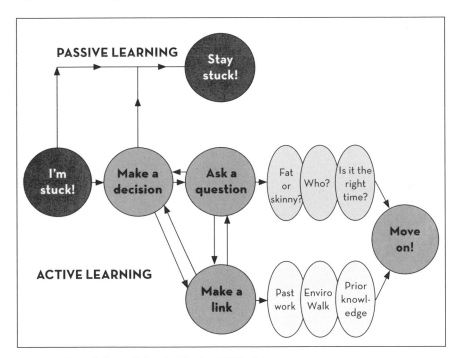

Source: adapted from Osler & Flack, 2008: 84

The moving-on map

The moving-on map is a model for learning that was developed with my Grades 2 and 3 students [seven to nine year olds]. The model was developed [as] a visual representation of the way students had learned to approach their learning. Terms such as passive and active learning, reflection, making decisions, staying stuck and Enviro Walk [a walk around the classroom environment to look at learning prompts] were common place and became important in the shared language of the classroom. It took my class about 45 minutes to construct the map [that] brought together the essential elements of the learning agenda of the class. After we had discussed, drafted and modified the map it was displayed as a poster in our classroom. The poster was a reminder as well as practical support for students as they went about their learning. The strength of the moving-on map lies in the talk and the nature of the work that had become part of the way students learned long before the map was created. Essentially they owned the process of their learning and the map was the culmination of what they already knew and valued. (Osler & Flack, 2008: 84)

Overview

This chapter offered a brief exploration of the notion of metacognition within the language and practice of teaching and learning. The language of metacognition is a reminder of the importance of encouraging pedagogic experiences to be structured in ways that foster the development of active, responsible learners. Metacognition is concerned with self-monitoring and self-regulating and so creates an expectation that practice will be thoughtfully designed in order to continually reinforce the value of questioning one's own thinking and learning.

Part 3
Professional Learning

Part 3 is designed to bring the ideas from the preceding sections together in terms of thinking about the ongoing development of teachers and teaching. The following chapters are conceptualised in such as way as to challenge notions of professional development, which are typically seen as telling teachers what to do, and to highlight the importance of professional learning—supporting teachers in directing their own knowledge growth. These chapters are designed to offer thoughts and actions that might be taken up within the profession in ways that will foster the ongoing development of teachers' specialist knowledge and skills. Becoming an accomplished teacher is about realising a personal vision for professional learning and enacting it in one's own practice.

10

Growing professional knowledge through reflection

The term 'reflection' is used a lot in education. It is commonly linked to ideas about learning and improvement in practice. However, like many ideas and concepts used in education, there is a certain degree of ambiguity in the use of terms that carry a common everyday meaning as well as a more specific meaning when attached to a particular field of endeavour. This clash between common and specific meanings could also account for some of the issues surrounding the notion of the theory–practice gap because, when a term is understood one way by some and differently by others, miscommunication is almost inevitable and so misunderstanding results. Reflection, it could well be argued, is an example of such a term.

Reflection defined

John Dewey (1933) introduced the notion of reflection to education many decades ago. However, even then it was clear that the term needed to be carefully defined in order to carry appropriate meaning: 'Reflective thinking, in distinction from other operations to which we apply the name of thought, involves (1) a state of doubt, hesitation, perplexity, mental difficulty, in which thinking originates, and (2) an active searching, hunting, inquiring, to find material that will resolve the doubt, settle and dispose of the perplexity' (Dewey, 1933: 12).

Dewey saw reflection as a method of challenging transmissive approaches to teaching because reflection highlighted the importance of understanding teaching as problematic. In so doing, he drew attention to the need for teachers to acknowledge that there is not necessarily one way of thinking or one way of responding to situations. Therefore, if there is not one true way of thinking, then our teaching methods need to support alternative ways of thinking and doing in order to develop students' learning for understanding. Learning for understanding is one form of thinking about what it means to be educated.

According to Dewey, reflection is a specialised form of thinking that a learner applies when confronted by a puzzling or curious situation in order to make better sense of that situation. He saw reflection as one of a teacher's artful skills which, when applied in practice: 'suppl[ies] the conditions that will arouse intellectual responses [in students]' (Dewey, 1933: 260). Dewey recognised that high-quality learning in schools did not occur in isolation and that teachers needed to create conditions that supported such learning. According to Dewey, creating favourable learning conditions results from teachers being reflective, and being reflective involves developing attitudes appropriate to supporting a reflective stance—in teachers and in students.

Attitudes

Dewey outlines three attitudes that he considered important in predisposing an individual to reflect. He continually demonstrates through his writing that it is not sufficient to 'know'; there also needs to be an accompanying desire to 'apply'. The attitudes which he described as important in securing the adoption and use of reflection are *open-mindedness*, *whole-heartedness* and *responsibility* (Loughran, 1996: 4).

Open-mindedness is evident through being open to new ideas and possibilities. Being open-minded means being prepared to listen to all sides and perspectives, particularly when they are contrary to one's own, and admitting that previously held views might have been wrong.

Whole-heartedness involves being enticed and engaged by ideas and thoughts: 'a teacher who arouses such an enthusiasm in his pupils has done something that no amount of formalized method, no matter how correct, can accomplish' (Dewey, 1933: 32).

Responsibility is associated with seeking meaning in that which has been learnt. It involves considering the consequences of actions and wanting to know why something is worth believing. If these attitudes are at the heart of reflection, then cultivating them becomes a worthy educational goal.

Dewey described reflection as being built on these three attitudes. However, he described reflection itself as a consequence of events comprising five elements: *suggestions, the problem, hypothesis, reasoning,* and *testing*. Each of the terms hints at their meaning. Suggestions are the ideas that come to mind when we are confronted by a puzzling or curious situation. The problem can be seen as a puzzling or curious situation that captures our attention but it is about a big-picture view, not just the intricate detail of the particular situation. Hypothesis involves thinking about what might be done and requires more careful observation of the situation in order to develop and refine understanding of the possibilities for action. Reasoning involves working through suggestions and hypotheses in order to think more carefully about how a possible response might be appropriate for the particular problem. Finally, testing is when the action decided upon is taken. Testing may support or negate the ideas and actions at hand but, importantly, failure is not mere failure. In reflection, failure is instructive because 'it either brings to light a new problem or helps to define and clarify the problem ... Nothing shows the trained thinker more than the use he makes of his errors and mistakes' (Dewey, 1933: 114).

Dewey's initial work created a reflective wave that continued to rise and fall over the ensuing decades. The notion of reflection made sense to many educationalists because learning through reflection on practice sits comfortably with ideas of developing expertise through experience. Although many people adapted and adjusted much of Dewey's work, the basic thrust of his descriptions of reflection remained relatively unchanged for a long period. But when Donald Schön (1983) offered an account of reflection based on his observations of professionals outside teaching, a new angle was introduced that created a whole new wave of interest in reflective practice.

Schön described two types of reflection: *reflection-on-practice* and *reflection-in-practice*. Reflection-on-practice was very similar to that described by Dewey: a deliberate process developed and purposely used to reconsider existing knowledge, beliefs, possibilities, ideas and actions. Reflection-in-action, on the other hand, was an almost subconscious process that experts developed and refined as a consequence of their learning through experience. This description of reflection-in-action immediately made sense to many professionals as it not only helped to account for how they functioned in the practice setting, but also offered insights into the tacit nature of knowledge of practice and why it can be so difficult to make that knowledge explicit for oneself and others.

Schön, like Dewey, recognised the importance of 'the problem' as a catalyst for reflection. He also described the problem, not in terms of it carrying negative connotations, but in terms of seeing a situation as being puzzling or curious or in some way inviting so that it attracted further (deeper) consideration. In this way Schön described the reflective practitioner as someone who looked again at the practice setting in order to see the problem from different perspectives (perhaps applying Dewey's attitude of open-mindedness). Hence, he described reflection as being based on an ability to appropriately frame the problem then, having done so, to reframe it and see the same problem in different ways.

Reflective practitioners are therefore thoughtful and well informed about their practice setting because they have built up their knowledge of that setting through learning from experience and being open to standing back and considering not only alternative ways of responding to a given situation, but of framing the situation in ways that acknowledge and respond to alternative perspectives. Being reflective, then, may appear quite simple and be an alluring tag to apply to our practice when considering situations from our own personal well-held positions. But when considered in relation to developing alternative perspectives through framing and reframing, reflection (and reflective practice) takes on a whole new meaning and is a much more demanding intellectual exercise because it is not about justifying practices and beliefs, it is about examining, learning and responding—something that can be particularly difficult and uncomfortable when the data does not support our own framing. Therefore, the use of the term 'reflection' can easily be misunderstood when applied to education—and more particularly to expertise in practice—because in everyday use reflection is mostly understood as the type of thinking associated with looking back and musing over something (often relatively fleetingly). However, as Dewey and Schön (among others) make clear, reflection is far from simple, is not fleeting, and calls on skills, knowledge and abilities to be used in a variety of challenging ways depending on the nature of the problem apprehended in the practice setting.

To further complicate the situation, a reflective practitioner who may be comfortable and capable in one practice setting may be seriously challenged when confronted by similar problems in a different or unfamiliar one. More so, the time of reflection (before, during or after) can also add another level of complexity to the nature and consequences of reflection. Therefore, being able to manage in the practice setting at different times in different ways while still being open to alternatives and to the necessary risk-taking at the heart of learning through experience is clearly demanding. Being a reflective practitioner requires much more than that which might be superficially understood through the everyday meaning of the term reflection. The reflective practitioner understands the importance of language as a basis for their professional knowledge of practice because it is crucial in shaping expertise and illustrates how such expertise draws on theory and practice in complementary rather than exclusive or contradictory ways. The following account illustrates Cate Baird's learning through reflection and highlights the reality of what it means to be a reflective practitioner. Baird's journal entries are noted in *italics*.

Learning through reflection on practice

Cate Baird

For a number of years I have been developing a need to partake in 'real and thought provoking' professional development, which would enable me to grow as a teacher and to encourage an active and self-motivated learning environment for my students. The more I read and searched for a forum to grow as a professional, the more I was returning to my own practice. After reading books and articles, I decided that to progress further I needed to investigate my own teaching and discover the themes and principles that directed my own practice. I realised I needed to collect honest data of my own teaching so that I could meaningfully analyse and reflect upon my teaching. To do this I recognised the need to become a reflective teacher and researcher, not only reflecting on daily incidents by recording them in a journal but also re-reading and analysing this journal and communicating the reflections to my colleagues, to share the knowledge from that learning with others.

One reason for me embarking on this task is that I believe teaching is a richly personal profession and yet, as teachers, we often look outside our vocation for training and guidelines to dictate our practice. I believe that it is time teachers paid more attention to their abilities to reflect, analyse and learn from their own practice and then to share these experiences with their peers—to develop our profession.

I started to keep a journal and to write in it after teaching a class. Over a period of time I started to see the benefits of constant journal writing. After reading my reflections I not only became aware of important issues in my teaching but also patterns and potential problems and perplexing situations in my day-to-day teaching that previously I perhaps too easily overlooked or dismissed. I needed to look again because I wanted to be the best teacher that I could be for both myself as a professional and for my students. Like most teachers I think that our students deserve the best teaching and learning environment that we can provide.

Establishing and maintaining a reflective journal

I decided to keep a journal to reflect on my teaching and to use as a data source for learning about my teaching and my students' learning; I wanted my focus to be on developing a better understanding of pedagogy. I maintained a detailed journal for a whole semester, starting at the beginning of the school year. I chose to write about one class of 27 Year 8 boys who were in my homegroup and whom I taught both Maths and Science.

I wrote in my journal after every class with the boys, writing down any incident that occurred during the lesson. At the beginning there was no pattern in my writing; I just re-enacted the lessons as I saw them from my teaching perspective, a daily reflection on my classroom practice. After a term of keeping this journal, I went back and started reading over the daily accounts. The strengths and weaknesses of my practice started to become increasingly apparent and themes stood out to me. This period of reflection became an eye-opening experience and a confronting time for me professionally. It was very disconcerting to find the number of frustrations and perplexing problems that were encountered with regularity; however, it was also wonderful to see the evidence over time of positive relationships being built and some building of students as active learners.

The overall trend of my journal became one of building networks of trusting relationships between me and the boys and the influences that affected or enhanced this process. The building of these relationships took time and constant effort and the journal illustrated how these were often hindered by aspects of teaching that appeared to be out of my immediate control.

The themes that repeatedly appeared throughout my journal were those linked to the principle of building and establishing positive relationships between myself and the students. Also prevalent was the theme of an environment where both teacher and students could feel safe to take risks as well as encouragement to enjoy and become engaged in the learning process. A final theme was related to the frustrations that constantly transpired to detract from a positive teaching and learning environment.

In order to illustrate how these themes emerged I offer the following account that I trust shows not only what I learnt but also how I learnt it and therefore what it means for my knowledge of practice.

Getting started

It is my belief that in order to be an effective and motivational teacher, a most important principle is to build positive relationships towards other individuals. I believe that as a teacher there is a need for students, parents or other members of staff to trust and respect my practice, hence, I must display a consistent and respectful approach towards others. I must build positive trusting relationships in the classroom. To do this I need to incorporate the following aspects into my practice: display an understanding of my students' backgrounds and individuality, show through listening and encouragement that all individuals' views matter and are important, and maintain a dynamic classroom where risk taking and responsibility for actions are seriously encouraged. As a reflective teacher I believe that an active learning environment can only occur once trust has been established among the group; but it's not always as simple as it sounds.

Before class:

First day of School. This journal will be my reflections on my Year 8 class of boys. I am to be these boys' homegroup teacher, and Maths and Science teacher. At present I only know two out of the 27 names on the class list, which will mean some interesting times ahead in terms of relationship and trust building over the next few weeks. I am so excited and have spent a fair amount of time during the holidays devising a variety of hands-on interactive classes aimed at increasing the engagement and enjoyment of learning.

First period I have the boys for Science, I have decided not to focus on science at all in this first period. The school has a code of conduct for students to follow; all homegroup teachers have been asked to remind classes about it. So my aim for this first lesson is to read through the code of conduct and discuss what it means for all of us and then get the boys and me to write our own code of conduct. I plan to give them some time to think about this and to write a list of things that are very important to each of them as an individual. Once I have seen this list I will direct the boys to place it in the front of their diaries for future reference. I have not planned further than this at this stage; we will just go with the flow.

After class:

WOW, talk about going with the flow. I had 27 'excited' boys, all doing their own thing, making a complete farce of the bonding and code of conduct lesson plan. They all wanted to outdo one another with holiday stories and tales of the completely impossible variety. This was not how I had envisaged starting a new year. I had forgotten how young boys aged twelve to fourteen could be, and there was no restraining their behaviour. I gave up trying to compete with the noise level of the whole class and instead went from group to group introducing myself and getting to know the boys' names and a little about them. I could then tell each small group about the code of conduct and instruct them to discuss their own within the group. I managed to inform all class members to complete their own code of conduct for homework and that we would discuss this in homegroup time tomorrow.

I had the boys again in sixth period for Maths. We were starting on looking at positive and negative numbers. I had planned to draw a number line on a piece of cardboard so the boys could put this into their workbooks to help them with the concept of adding together positive and negative numbers. I had planned for this to take about half the period and then spend the rest of the time doing a few examples together as a class, hopefully being able to pick up on some names and some of the skill levels within the class. (Oh, I wish I knew some more names!) Again, as in this morning's class, the noise level was almost unbearable. I still cannot ascertain if this noise was of the good or destructive kind. I for one could not hear myself think, so I ended up yelling above the noise and displaying my wrath in the form of a thorough dressing down and explanation of what is appropriate in a learning classroom and behaviour that is better left in the school grounds, etc. All at the top of my voice. I HATE doing this, I feel out of control when I act in this manner in front of a class, and I am uncertain as to whether the results are ever satisfactory. We did not achieve much learning today. I had great plans . . .

As you can see, my first day was certainly frustrating. I really had to struggle to keep the day in perspective. I had made long-term plans that required building up trust and developing an understanding of each student's interests and skills and somehow forgot that this only happens with little steps. I should not have expected instant results.

My reaction was to review my lesson plan for the next day and adopt a more conservative approach.

We had Maths first period. I got the boys to get out their number lines and without further discussion got them doing exercises from their textbook. My only direction was, 'If you are having trouble put your hand up and if you find this work too easy put your hand up'. Then I proceeded to walk around the room interacting with different groups. I know from past experience that this sort of lesson keeps the students busy and on task and allows me an opportunity to relate one-on-one or in small groups. However, I go into these sorts of textbook-directed classes with a real sense of disappointment because I believe that it is a non-challenging form of teaching and I am unsure as to the amount of learning that really occurs. Having said that I remember as a student really enjoying this type of Maths lesson as I could work at my own pace and develop my own understanding. It also meant if I had a specific problem I could get the teacher to help me in a one-to-one manner.

Showing interest: supporting learning

It is my very strong belief that as a teacher I need to show interest in each individual student and develop an understanding of their background. That way, I might have a better chance of reaching my students and encouraging them as learners. Self-esteem and confidence play a huge role in the learning process; if a student believes that they are valued and safe in a learning environment then often increased self-esteem and a more active role and responsibility for learning follow.

The boys had completed making their parachutes [a task I had set for a lesson on air resistance] and we had dropped them from small distances but they really wanted to be able to drop them from a great height. The only safe place to do this in the school was from the locked window of a storage room above the gym. So I organised with the Principal to do this. The boys had a fantastic time dropping and modifying their chutes, and they also got to see the Principal in another light as he helped them with modifications and made suggestions.

I handed over the reins to the individuals that posed the questions in the discussion. These guys led the class in trying out their experiments. This session lasted about ten minutes, until the bell went and even then I had to push them out the door to their next class.

I have found that it is a very difficult task to really understand the learning needs of all students. Some tend to hide their learning difficulties behind aggressive, anti-social or disruptive behaviour. Pride is a major factor to consider and so to establish relationships I need to go slowly and maintain a consistently positive and open approach. To do this within a classroom setting is often difficult and sometimes the things we do as teachers detract from our initial goal. By displaying a positive and caring manner, though, there is a possibility that foundations for trust might be established. If so, those students who require assistance may well be encouraged to seek it from the teacher they trust.

I had two boys in for lunch detention today. They were supposed to be working on an overdue assignment. I was sitting at the table with them working on a unit on forces. I started playing with some magnets, super-strong ones, to work out an activity with them. The two guys became really interested and asked if they could help, so together we got out all the magnet activities and they started to assist in devising activities and asking all sorts of relevant questions regarding magnetism. When it came time for their detention to end they did not want to go; so they stayed to create a fantastic unit of activities based on magnets, including questions to answer, which they partially wrote up on my laptop. Learning can be so simple when engaged.

A boy that had been a real behaviour problem worked really well in class today when I put him in a new group. He left the room almost strutting when I told him that I was really proud of his behaviour today.

It's not easy to assess every student's learning needs. Sometimes little things make a difference and lead to learning that was not planned (as in the journal entries above); at other times there needs to be some structure to help. To facilitate ease of communication between students and myself I decided to instigate 'learning diaries'.

The learning diary is an idea I have had for a long time; however, I have never implemented one before. The idea is to write at the end of every lesson in the back of their science workbook a brief statement on what they learnt or did not understood in the lesson. I said they could complete it in any manner they wanted, they could draw ideas or events if they wanted, and they could claim that they learnt nothing this lesson. We discussed this idea as a class. Then I told them that the reason I wanted them to do this was so that they had a record of their learning and that they could then start taking responsibility for that learning. I also told them that I would be regularly checking this diary to pick up on problems that they may be having, and that they could use it to show me that they understood the work as we were doing it—use their diary to explain the different concepts covered. The boys liked this idea so we decided to trial it for a while and see how it went.

The boys wrote some interesting comments in their learning diaries. The object of the lesson though is not always what they learn: for example, 'Silicon looks like a shiny metal and that's what they put in boobs to make them bigger'.

The learning diaries became an invaluable source of information, not only giving me insights into what the boys learnt but also into their misconceptions, interests and abilities. As a teacher I feel a constant need to devise methods of getting individuals to be involved in class discussions and activities without putting any individual in an awkward or embarrassing position in front of their peers. To give freely of individual ideas can be seen as a great risk by many students and this can require a dramatic change in mindset. I think the learning diaries helped to create new ways of encouraging this sort of risk taking because many students had already 'spoken up' to me in their diaries so I learnt how to build on this in classroom work more generally.

The discussion that resulted was really good but loud. It was also directed by only about a third of the class. A couple of the groups had no input at all, even though I had received some fantastic observations from them individually. So I started to tell the class some of these observations. I said that David had a great idea about 'the smoke being dense or thick enough for the heat from the flame to travel back to the wick'. I was hoping that by giving public recognition in a positive manner these 'quiet' individuals would feel more at ease in adding their ideas in future. This approach did not work well in all cases. In fact in a couple of cases the guys just seemed really embarrassed, but by the end of the discussion at least two-thirds of the class had been involved in some manner. While the discussion was occurring I was writing down some of the points of interest on the board and I said that anyone who wanted to write down this work in their books could do so at the end of the discussion. About half the class chose to do this.

I have come to understand that accepting responsibility for learning and allowing others to learn is a real skill. I feel that as a teacher, although I know this, it is not always quite so easy to ensure I am doing it with my students. Developing teaching and learning this way can take a long time and requires risk taking and flexibility on the part of both the teacher and the students.

As usual the guys all gathered around the front desk while the demonstration was performed. This was done twice. The whole time the guys were asking questions. The only ones that I answered, however, were those that dealt with the equipment. I left all other questions open, which frustrated the boys at times; however, after a while other class members came up with answers, and often these were well thought out. I really must remember to allow this non-teacher-directed discussion to occur with greater regularity. Through the discussion a couple of the boys came up with some great variations on the theme.

My aim as a teacher is to establish and maintain a positive learning environment that encourages active engagement with ideas. In order to do this, students need to be encouraged to explore, investigate, discuss and openly question ideas and issues within the content being learnt. I believe that engagement and enjoyment result from being a flexible teacher willing to take risks.

[One] episode had completely diverted us from the lesson plan. However, I love this sidetracking and I think the boys get more out of this sort of lesson than me directing all their learning. I started the Predict-Observe-Explain (POE) on 'fast reactions'. Two of the boys wanted to do the demonstration so I told them what to do and they did the experiment. It was great! I thought that this would take about five minutes and they would all tell me how boring science is. They all crowded around the front desk watching this demonstration, all getting more excited at each stage. It was difficult to get the boys to sit down at the end of the demonstration because they all wanted to add more sugar or water, or do more stirring, to see what would happen next.

To build an active learning environment I saw the need to take risks and respond to the challenges in teaching and learning as they occurred in a lesson. I also found that when handled appropriately, risk taking encouraged the building of trust, allowed for a safer learning environment and encouraged more students to be engaged in, and enjoy, their learning.

Of course, it's not all as easy as it may sound. I had many daily struggles and frustrations and found that these consumed a lot of my time and energy. When caught up in the rush and bustle of teaching, more often than not the successes too easily become lost. I noticed how my reflections could sometimes become very focused on these problems, overshadowing the other aspects of my practice disproportionately. Through this project, I have come to better understand some of my teaching frustrations. Their causes have become a challenge for me as they inevitably impact on my teaching as well as my responses to the students' learning.

Classroom management and responsibility for learning
Establishing relationships with students is important to me. In
order to build these with individuals and groups I have found that
consistent, positive reinforcement over a period of time is the most
appropriate approach for my teaching style and for the building of
self-esteem and learning outcomes for my students. The students
continually test the boundaries and sometimes these can clash with
attempts at building relationships. This can be very frustrating.

*After lunch, we had Maths again. I had devised an activity to
hopefully keep the boys engaged and interested. We were going
to do maps and scales today. Each boy was given a plastic pocket
filled with three local maps, one piece of string and a ruler, and brief
instructions and questions to answer. Most of the class was late and
it took quite some time to hand out their package to each student.
The boys were so noisy and disruptive, out of seats, yelling at one
another, throwing paper balls all around the room and completely
carrying on. Only about half of the boys got on task at all during
this lesson. My management skills lacked greatly. The class was a
nightmare and even the boys I can usually rely on were noisy and
disruptive—pack mentality.*

*I had the boys second period. I have thought a lot about the
'change' that occurred in the class dynamics yesterday afternoon.
We need to wipe the slate clean. I cannot allow this disruptive
behaviour to keep going. I started the class by saying, 'Yesterday
was disappointing. Learning time was wasted. We will forget all
about previous behaviours and start again.'*

At times the reasons behind the disruptive behaviour may
be clear but the skills required to rectify the situation may be
elusive and so it can be very frustrating. I had a very perplexing
time trying to change the boys' attitude and conduct during Maths
classes. They thought Maths should be organised and run in a very
formalised non-threatening manner; activities that required active
involvement were not part of their way of seeing Maths being
conducted.

*We had Maths first period. As a group these boys can be
so noisy, which is the main feedback that I am getting from all of
their other teachers. I generally can tolerate noise in a classroom
when I consider the noise to be productive. However, these guys*

go beyond that limit time and time again. In Science the noise is an illustration of their engagement and enjoyment but in Maths classes I am struggling. I have tried a variety of methods for delivering the information using all of the techniques I incorporate in Science classes. At present, however, the only way I have found for getting the majority to work productively is to set work out of their textbook or sheets and go around the room explaining questions to individuals or small groups. If I deviate from this method into a more practical approach or a discussion or problem-solving activity, the class goes to top volume and becomes unbearable.

We finally started Maths. I am really teaching Maths so differently to how I would like to. I do not understand why the class dynamics change so dramatically from one subject to the other. It does not make sense. The guys pulled out their Maths books and proceeded to work on the next exercise, putting up their hands when they encountered difficulties. About two-thirds are happy working this way; the other third, most of whom have great difficulty in Maths or in reading the information, usually just sit there looking bored or getting increasingly disruptive. I am at a loss as to how to tackle this—it has me so perplexed!

Trying to change the learning environment too quickly with some groups of students only leads to 'pack revolt' and extreme frustration. Often the go-softly approach can work better for class-management tactics, but leaves you very frustrated about the learning process. Classroom-management skills are often the cause of much stress and anxiety among teachers, and I now see that until I have established relationships the go-softly approach causes the least trouble.

I believe there is a need for learning to be less formal, more enjoyable, integrated, relevant to the learner, encouraging, and concentrating less on the acquisition of knowledge and more on the development and socialisation of the individual and their potential as a learner. Individual students need to take responsibility for their own learning. In order for students to be motivated they need to be engaged in the process of learning and in the content of the learning. Some students engage in tasks naturally as they link concepts and see relevance or subconsciously accept that the process of learning has many facets to develop and understand.

These students can usually motivate themselves regardless of the teacher or teaching style. For others, though, the motivation comes not so much from the process of learning and understanding but from the positive rewards that are achieved from doing a task well. The teacher has a large role to play with the learning of such students as this type of student responds to a teacher's directions and looks for any signals to achieve a more positive result.

Many students cannot see the relevance of learning certain subjects or areas of content. It appears they require an understanding of the purpose of the subject before they can attempt to become engaged. For the teacher, then, there is a need to recognise this and encourage them to respond to their right to question and, to the best of their ability, explain the reasons for learning the content and the relevance it has to their lives. However, this is not a simple task. Other students may never see the relevance and refuse to become engaged and can often end up being very disruptive. It is this minority who can be the most frustrating members of a class, making the teaching and learning process very difficult.

The teacher's role is made all the more difficult when students' behaviour inhibits access to the learning and the ideas of a subject. It can be exceptionally frustrating to have to restart the learning each lesson and to try and move the students from one set of physical behaviours to another of cognitive behaviours. One of the major difficulties is helping students come to accept some responsibility for their own learning.

[A] resulting discussion was okay, however, I received many comments such as these gems: 'You are the teacher; you should be telling us, not us telling you', and 'We are not learning anything; we are telling you the answers we already know'. It was very hard not to stop and justify my actions and teaching strategies at times—I did not want the boys to become frustrated or disheartened by my actions.

However, after [an] experiment I asked a few of the class what they believed had occurred and not one member could tell me! Then I asked, 'What does this H_2O mean?' Blank stares looked back at me, so on the board I underlined the H in one colour and the O in another and asked about each letter in turn. Eventually they came up with hydrogen and oxygen, mainly through my direction, because I felt I was beginning to lose some interest.

When students do not appear to accept responsibility for their own learning, it seems that it then becomes too easy for the teacher to allow them to be dependent learners, yet that is not the intention. For example, through this project I have noticed that I often try to justify my teaching approaches and give too much direction in class. The reason for this, I think, is that I am trying to prevent the class, or individual students, from becoming disillusioned or losing self-esteem. However, I often repeat this behaviour with great regularity so the class tend to rely upon it, resulting in a lack of student motivation if the task gets too difficult or confronting. This can be very frustrating as I am equally a part of the problem as the solution.

Students that struggle with learning, for whatever reason, are often the most frustrating to deal with in a classroom environment. Such students feel inadequate and tend to act out disruptive behaviours in order to get attention, or sometimes become very insular, isolated and uncommunicative. These students tend to take up a lot of the teacher's time, sometimes to the detriment of the rest of the class and the process of learning. I have found that most of these students are so used to feeling 'dumb', and since the only form of attention they have received in school is negative they are almost immune to punishment; it is a part of their role.

One of these young gentlemen, however, really concerned me. He has been of concern for some time and I have tried talking with him one-on-one a number of times but I do not know how best to assist him. He has a numeracy/literacy level of grade 1 and his attitude to school (not surprisingly) is awful. He wants to leave but he so desperately craves attention he will do almost anything to get it. He believes he can leave school without many educational skills, get a job and earn big dollars and be happy. He ended up in tears again, mainly through frustration, I think, so I kept him behind after the others left.

I have found this type of student the hardest to deal with in a consistent manner as they often place me in an awkward position with regard to the rest of the class, as other students believe that it is one rule for the disruptive students and another for the ones who do the right thing. There is always a strong sense of wanting to justify your actions to the rest of the class as the behaviour-management techniques are often not performed in front of the others but often take up a lot of time after class. Other students do not always see it this way.

I kept ten boys in after the lunch bell for about fifteen minutes, to have a chat about behaviour and what is appropriate. We talked about learning and I asked them in a casual manner what learning meant to each of them. Most of the boys responded to this really well and told me all the things that they considered to be important to learning and a learning environment. Then they told me how they had disrupted that environment and what they could try to change. They all appeared to be genuinely upset that they had annoyed me, and that I was taking away their lunch time too. I took out their codes of conduct that they had written at the beginning of the year and marked them all with one big cross. Two crosses result in an after-school detention. I do not know how productive our discussions were. Time will tell.

I have a group of boys that have very low numeracy and literacy skills. This has led on many occasions to really frustrating teaching and learning episodes. Assisting students is demanding and time consuming and other commitments often dictate the level of effectiveness. There is also a constant need to be aware of the 'you're not fair, it's my turn' chorus from the rest of the class, when dedicating too much time and effort to some students. It becomes a frustrating task trying to teach to completely different skill levels while still maintaining a consistent, engaging, flexible approach to learning. This is exacerbated when it comes to assessment.

I took four of them to a side 'prac' bench, and asked them to record their observations in a series of simple drawings. Once they did this I asked them to explain briefly why they thought this happened and I quickly wrote this down for them. I do not know how to assist these guys—school must be so frustrating. I have read a lot on integration of multi-learning levels; however, I am yet to see this work successfully for all involved.

About ten of the guys are completely computer illiterate, seven because they cannot read the information, and the remainder due to the confusing instructions. They refuse to stop and listen. When I am explaining to the whole class, they want me to explain it to them individually. I am slowly running out of patience. I need them to listen to instructions as a group as I cannot clone myself. (God, how do primary teachers do it? SHOW INDEPENDENCE, GUYS.)

I had a test for the boys today. It is so hard writing a fair test to span all the levels of ability in a class. I understand that testing is a requirement but I do not want them to make it into a full-on competition, especially given the different skill levels we are working from. I do not want to quash the self-esteem of the struggling kids. I want to be in a position to give them positive reinforcement for their efforts (for all those who deserve it) as well as making the test difficult enough to challenge those who need challenging. I decided to make the test open-book (their work book only) and to give them all a chance to work to the best of their abilities. Much of their test was based on the knowledge gleaned from POEs and experiments. I tried to keep the writing to a minimum, due to quite a number of the boys not being able to read the information, and I included a lot of diagrams to assist these kids. Most of the boys took the full period to complete the test, and some went into the second period. Three handed in their tests after about five minutes. I directed them to try to do some Maths work, as they had their Maths books. All of these boys have approximately grade 1–2 literacy level. HOW CAN I HELP THEM?????

Frustration is a strong theme in teaching. I have come to see that frustrations have underlying causes and impact on teaching as well as some of the associated actions that come with the teaching role. It is so difficult to maintain a sense of professional accomplishment when working towards helping students attempt to become better learners when so many things frustrate attaining that goal. It may well be that the manner in which teachers respond to frustration is by inadvertently being inflexible and uncompromising as the need to feel in control clouds one's judgement and actions. To be the best teacher I can requires me to stay calm and relaxed and to not be overtaken by the need to always be in control.

Learning about myself as a teacher
The children are why I teach. As I have worked with teenagers over the years there have been many occasions when I lost track of the most important reason for teaching and for being a teacher: the children. The content, the manner in which I teach, and the administration, are all on the periphery and incorporated into the relationships I build with my students. I have had many colleagues tell me that I care too much about the welfare and happiness of my

students, that we should only be concerned about the students' learning and discipline. I am also of the belief that to enable individual students to realise their potential they need to trust and respect their teacher(s) as a person. The reason for my convictions is interesting—it's because it just feels right. In these times when things feel right my students appear to appreciate my efforts. That is how I would like to be regarded by them in order to feel safe enough to take risks and to become active and self-motivated in my learning. So why would my students be any different?

As I have worked through my journal I have started to reflect on the strengths and weaknesses in my practice. I began to develop a sense of the underlying principles that guided my everyday practice. Before embarking on this journey of professional discovery I believed I was a reflective person. I was always concerned about how I taught to encourage and promote student-generated learning. I know that in the everyday running of schools teachers generally find little time to reason through why they teach in the manner they do. More often than not it is probably a gut feeling or it is how they have always taught—consequently it is easy to rationalise one's practice and see no need to change. Conducting this project has helped me to challenge my taken-for-granted assumptions and views and see the need to better understand what I do and why, to make the tacit in my practice much more explicit, both for myself and in trying to talk about and explain my teaching to others.

I now think that what we miss out on in teaching is the importance of self-study and reflection on practice. They should be integral aspects of all teachers' practice as it is a major source of professional development. Teacher knowledge is the *most* important form of knowledge in the profession. Teachers need to empower themselves and their peers to place much more relevancy and importance in sharing and communicating their goals, principles and themes underlying their individual practice; this knowledge can be obtained from nowhere else but from teachers themselves.

This reflective self-study is based on a period of teaching a class of 27 boys. It has shown me that the most important principle in my practice is *establishing and maintaining a positive relationship within the classroom*. The building of trust, through a consistent, nurturing and respectful manner, creates for the students (and the teacher) a safe and active learning environment. This, for me, is what teaching is about. This project has helped me to see this and to explicitly work towards developing a greater understanding about how I do that. This project has helped me to begin to develop my professional knowledge in teaching and, through writing it up, to begin to articulate and share it with others. My understanding of what I do, and how and why, is now different to what it was when I started out on this journey. This has been for me very powerful professional development: something I couldn't gain from those after-school sessions when I'm tired and worried about tomorrow's classes—and certainly not something I could be told by a guru. I needed the time, the space and the support to look at what I did and to honestly learn about myself and the way I try to support my students' learning.

I now have a heightened sense of awareness of the knowledge of reflection and have come to see and understand teaching and the teaching profession differently through this process. Reflecting on the teaching and learning environment and recognising the strengths and weaknesses in my practice, which were not evident prior to the commencement of this study, I now see teaching as much more problematic and revolving more around dilemmas of practice. Through maintaining a journal, and with further reflection after the completion of the journal, I have been able to identify the principles and themes that direct my practice in ways that were not evident to me when I was caught up in the daily busyness of the world of teaching. Further to this, my study probably caused me to focus on problems which now, in hindsight, caught more attention in analysis than I had probably intended. Yet this is the nature of thinking about teaching—being attracted to the difficulties rather than the successes of practice.

I now think that a feature of an effective self-study is that the teacher sees themselves as part of the problem and accepts a deal of responsibility for the classroom environment. As a teacher I learnt from this study more about the sense of responsibility afforded in a classroom, while also recognising the need to allow students to take on more of that responsibility for themselves. In my practice I have used the knowledge gained from this experience to influence my current approach to practice—an important knowledge gain that is not always recognisable in the staid text of a traditional research project. This is evidenced to me in allowing for greater student involvement and responsibility in the classroom setting, hence allowing for enhanced risk taking by my students and myself.

I have been in a position both within my school and in external teacher forums to share the experience gained from this project and to therefore discuss with other professionals some of the strategies and difficulties encountered along the way. Similarly, I have been asked for, and received, both formal and informal feedback from colleagues, which has allowed me to further my own professional development and open up new possibilities for other teachers to think about their practice.

I am now aware of the areas in my practice that I would like to further study and gain help in through specific professional development. These are the areas that will add meaning and value to my personal teaching experiences and most importantly the learning skills and outcomes of my students. This is also consistent with a growing need to enhance the teaching and learning process overall and to pay more attention to the importance of keeping the profession relevant to our students, parents and community, and an ability to communicate these understandings with colleagues.

As a result of conducting this study I would now strongly argue for the use of self-study and reflection on practice so that it can lead to greater sharing of teachers' knowledge and be seen as an important form of professional development. I believe that empowerment and authority would then be given to teachers in ways that might allow genuine responsibility for the direction and implementation of one's own professional growth to be realised. It is only after such a reflective process that I believe I can honestly and reliably assess my personal practice and use that knowledge to further grow as a professional in the demanding world of teaching.

As Baird's reflective account above illustrates, her ability to frame and reframe the practice setting changes dramatically according to what she sees in that setting. As a consequence, that which she apprehends as a problem, and the ways in which she responds, are influenced by what she learns as a consequence of looking in from different perspectives. She does not rationalise her behaviour or seek to justify her actions; rather, she is intent on developing a deeper understanding of the situation and so responds in a much more informed and thought-ful manner. The tests (as per Dewey's elements of reflection) that she experiments with in her classes do not always come up with solutions to the problem (much less the *correct* solution), but in reflecting on her practice she illustrates how expertise is derived from seeing teaching as being problematic and seeking to better understand peda-gogy—the teaching and learning relationship.

Overview

This chapter illustrated how learning from experience is dependent on reflection on experience and that reflection involves much more than simply thinking about a situation, episode or event. Reflection is a specialised form of thought that lies at the heart of professional practice. Through reflection on experience, teachers' knowledge of practice is developed and enhanced in ways that help to inform and shape their expertise. As Cate Baird's account in this chapter made clear, through formalising her reflection on practice she came to see herself, her prac-tice and her understanding of professional learning differently. Her reflective account offers genuine insights into what it means to be an expert pedagogue.

11

The value of teacher research

As has been noted a number of times in this book, the perceived gap between theory and practice tends to lead to polarised views of teaching. When viewed from these opposing positions, theory is sometimes seen as unhelpful in practice while practice is sometimes characterised as atheoretical. These differences are most starkly evident in the stereotype of teaching as doing, in which teachers are only seen as teaching when in the classroom directing students' learning. Unfortunately, thinking about teaching as doing ignores many other aspects of teaching that are important in shaping the quality of practice, many of which are not immediately evident in this stereotypically narrow view of teaching. Cate Baird's account in the previous chapter highlights many of these other aspects crucial to the quality of teaching. Bridging the theory–practice gap is important so that the complexity of teaching and learning can be opened up for examination and analysis, the outcomes of which better inform pedagogical practices.

One way of bridging the theory–practice gap is through the work of teacher researchers. Teacher researchers are both practitioners and theoreticians. They bring to bear their expert knowledge of the practice setting in the development of the conceptual underpinnings of their research. Teacher researchers tend to be primarily concerned with better understanding how their practice influences their students' learning and, in so doing, their studies offer new and insightful ways of understanding pedagogy and the quality of practice.

Teacher research is not new, but in recent times it has attracted more attention as shifts in understanding of the nature of research have led to greater acceptance of the importance of formulating research questions, methods and analytic approaches to researching teaching and learning that are more sensitive to practice. Further to this, arguments about the nature of knowledge, and its relationship with practice, have further highlighted the value of teacher research because what teachers know, need to know and are able to do is understood very differently when examined from a teacher's perspective, as opposed to that of an external observer.

In fact, teaching and research, like theory and practice, should not be regarded as separate and discrete entities, but should be seen as complementary because 'it is difficult to see how teaching can be improved or how curricula proposals can be evaluated without self-monitoring on the part of teachers. A research tradition, which is accessible to teachers and which feeds teaching must be created if education is to be significantly improved' (Stenhouse, 1975: 165). This observation is no less important today.

The growth of teacher research is partly as a result of advocates such as Marilyn Cochran-Smith and Susan Lytle (1999; 2004; Lytle & Cochran-Smith, 1991), who recognised that teachers' ways of knowing are quite different to that ascribed to in more traditional educational research. They recognised that teachers' learning about teaching *and* learning is inevitably based on their classroom experiences. As such, teachers have a privileged position in terms of understanding classroom dynamics and other crucial aspects of pedagogy that dramatically shape what they see in practice as well as what they want to know more about. Therefore, the types of questions and inquiries that teachers tend to pursue in their classrooms with their students are fundamentally different to those that might be considered important by those not so familiar with, and responsible for, the teaching and learning environment. Advocates for teacher research have helped to focus renewed attention on the teacher's perspective and have been important in supporting not only what is researched but also how that research is reported.

Research audience

It has long been recognised that a large proportion of educational research does not necessarily speak to us as teachers. There are many reasons for this, not least of which is the fact that many researchers write for their own academic audience, not a teacher audience, and so although their research outcomes may ostensibly have much to say to teachers, the lack of connection to the profession diminishes its overall impact on teachers and their practice.

Teacher research is generally constructed and portrayed in ways that we find more accessible and engaging and so offers possibilities for bridging the theory-practice gap and opening up understandings of each other. Because it is embedded in issues and concerns drawn from classroom practice, this research tends to examine topics and situations that we as teachers identify with and therefore are interested in reading and better understanding. Teacher research does not set out to always be conducted in ways that might be generalisable; rather, it seeks to be conducted and portrayed in such a way that others might readily identify with the situations described and so create an invitation to consider the research outcomes in relation to their own context. It is this ability to identify with the problems, issues and concerns of other teachers in similar situations that is an initial allure in teacher research because of the possibility that new ideas and approaches to teaching and learning might be gleaned from someone else's work. In so doing, we might then be able to better adapt, adjust and apply that in our own practice—to find or develop something that will work in class tomorrow.

Although we are continually developing and testing ideas about teaching and learning in our classrooms, such inquiry is not usually formalised and so we do not automatically link what we are doing, in exploring and developing deeper understandings of pedagogy, with research. However, it is not such a large step to move from informal inquiry into teaching and learning to the development of more concrete research questions and application of appropriate procedures for collecting data to help shed new light on those questions.

Fred Korthagen et al. (2001) describe formal knowledge (*episteme*) as theory with a 'big T' and practical knowledge (*phronesis*) as theory with a 'small t'. He does so partly to demonstrate that theory and practice can be bridged by thinking about theory along a continuum from 'big T' to 'small t' and by considering how the nature of theory matters in terms of how it is linked to practice. Thinking about theory in this way is also helpful in terms of understanding research (what it does, how and why). The more traditional, large-scale, externally controlled and conducted studies could be thought of as research with a 'big R', and teacher research—the more specific, personal insider examination of practice—as research with a 'small r'. That does not mean that one is more important than the other but acknowledges that they can serve different purposes, although those purposes may very well converge at times depending on the catalyst for the research and the manner in which the results are intended to influence the nature of practice.

Initiating teacher research

Just as a problem can act as a catalyst for reflection, so too there needs to be an issue, concern or question that creates the incentive for embarking on a teacher research project. We are too busy in our daily practice to pursue additional work unless it serves a worthwhile purpose in terms of our teaching and/or our students' learning. In the normal course of events, we share our understanding of practice through the teaching procedures and activities we use in our classrooms. Typically, our evaluations revolve around our perceptions of how our teaching influences the quality of student learning. When experimenting with new or different teaching procedures we tend to have a heightened sense of awareness about the nature of the pedagogical experience. However, as noted above, there is a difference between how we might feel about a given situation, and actually collecting data in order to seek evidence on which to base particular conclusions. Therefore, there is a difference between that which might trigger our reconsidering practice as opposed to researching that practice.

We share much of our thinking about practice through the stories and experiences we have of teaching. We discuss how we do things, the types of responses we get from students and the ways in which we adjust and change our practice as a result of what we learn through experience. These episodes can become a trigger for considering a situation in more detail. Triggers for teacher research may be captured and portrayed through the use of what Max van Manen (1999) described as anecdotes. Anecdotes can be seen as the instances in daily practice that capture a teacher's attention. Through documenting and sharing anecdotes, others may be encouraged to reflect on their own practice and that can also act as a trigger for deeper exploration of issues and concerns through teacher research. The following is an example of an anecdote written by a student teacher that invites further questioning of practice.

What you hear in silence

This was the first time I taught this particular Year 10 class. The topic was melody writing and I was more than prepared for the lesson with every word scripted and carefully emblazoned on the pages in front of me in my lesson plan.

'Okay, melody writing is a fairy simple concept,' I started, 'as long as you follow the seven rules.'

'Rule number one is . . .' and so I started blurting out the rules as the class frantically raced to write them down in their notebooks.

'And rule number seven, are you with me now, James?' my confidence growing with every word as I pushed them to keep up. 'You must *always* end on the tonic.'

It was as easy as that! I knew that now all they had to do was follow the rules and they would all be melody writers extraordinaire.

'And for homework tonight I want you to follow those rules and write your own melody. Any questions?' I asked as I scanned the room quite pleased with my delivery.

The silence beckoned so I asked again, 'Okay, quite simple really. Any questions?'

Not a sound.

'Great, they all understand,' I said to myself in a congratulatory tone.

The bell sounded right on cue and as the students filed out of the room I started to pack up my things to follow them out.

I was pleased with today's lesson and was quietly rewarding myself on a job well done as I strode to the door.

'Did you understand any of that?' Ben asked Jeff as they spilled out into the corridor.

'Nup, not one bit,' Jeff said.

'Me either.' (quoted in Loughran, 2006: 130)

This anecdote illustrates how easy it can be to view the success or otherwise of a lesson from only one perspective and how misleading that perspective can be when not checked against alternative sources. In this case, the student teacher was concerned about delivering the key aspects of the lesson and had perhaps overlooked what delivery really means when translated in terms of student learning. As the anecdote demonstrates, the sense of self-satisfaction that can accompany trouble-free delivery of information can be quite seductive and, in some cases, makes it difficult to see what else is happening in a pedagogical episode. Through this anecdote the student teacher illustrated how overhearing a couple of students' honest responses to what they had just experienced broke down a barrier and encouraged him to stop and think again about what had really happened. But you do not have to be a student teacher to experience such a situation. We are all confronted by occasions when our delivery feels good but the expected student learning does not follow. The real issue is being aware that it is happening.

If we are aware of such a situation, then an anecdote such as the one above could easily be a trigger for a teacher research project based on the fundamental question of: 'How do we come to recognise when we are telling instead of teaching?' As a consequence of posing that question, it is almost inevitable that it will be followed up with: 'What do I do about it?'

In teacher research, the initial inquiry commonly leads to the need for action. Hence, results derived from questioning a pedagogical situation almost always lead to deeper considerations of what to do as a consequence. From a teaching perspective, there is little point in becoming more informed about our practice if appropriate change does not follow. Our professional satisfaction is intimately tied to the quality of student learning and how the latter is achieved demands constant attention. While the rhetoric of teaching for understanding sounds good and flows easily from the tongue, the reality is much more difficult. It is in the types of dilemmas highlighted through the anecdote above that teacher research projects are so often born.

Anecdotes also offer a reminder of the problematic nature of teaching. Teaching is problematic because dilemmas are at the heart of practice and they are not solved—they are managed. The quality of practice, then, is evident in the expertise associated with managing those dilemmas, and good teachers make that management look easy. In order to better understand the expertise that underpins quality practice, articulation of professional knowledge matters. Teacher research offers ways of explicating that knowledge.

Doing teacher research

A common catalyst for teacher research is the goal of improved classroom practice, but it is a big step to move from thinking about practice to more formally researching it because there is little encouragement or reward associated with that effort. Unfortunately, teacher research is an additional task on top of our existing classroom demands and so requires a commitment that extends beyond the normal expectations of teaching. However, for many involved in teacher research the rewards that flow as a consequence tend to create a momentum that encourages further interest in exploring the nature of the professional knowledge of practice.

Researching writing workshops

As an experienced Grade 3 teacher, Jim Swaim (2004) found himself looking again at what was happening with his students in their classroom writing workshops:

> After a short teacher-directed mini-lesson, the children write silently for 10 minutes. For the next 20 minutes they have the choice of continuing to write, working on drafts, publishing, or having a conference with a teacher or peer. In a peer conference, the author chooses a partner, and reads her/his story out loud and decides, with the partner's input, what type of changes could be made. The last 10 minutes of the workshop is a class sharing session where an author shares his/her writing piece with the entire class . . . The hope is that by experiencing the roles of both writer and audience, the authors' decision to publish or not would be an informed one. (Swaim, 2004: 71)

Swaim's concern for developing his students' writing led him to ask the question, 'How do children connect through their writing and what constitutes an honest response to their writing?' As a starting point for his research he decided to audiotape students' peer conferences as a way of collecting data on how the students worked together in their conference roles. It didn't take long before he found himself questioning not only his students' approach to learning but also his approach to teaching.

When listening to the audiotape of two students in their writing conference he was struck by the way the students seemed to be using the language of revision he had emphasised in a mini–lesson and felt as though their need to use the language had actually created a barrier to their understanding. Both students seemed well versed in the language of revision but did not appear to translate that language into meaning in terms of knowledge about how to revise. This led him to see that both he and his students had been too concerned with displaying the revision routines, which meant that when they put them into practice the focus was more about delivering a script than developing deeper understanding through the text. From this he concluded that the actual process of revision had been dramatically reduced and that his students were no longer responding to the content of the stories on their own terms. In other words, their use of the procedural language got in the way of natural and honest conversation about the writing.

Having recognised this situation in the peer conferences, he decided to listen more carefully to the manner in which students spoke to one another during class sharing. In one particular session, two students sat in the author's chair and presented their first draft of a picture book they had been working on together to the rest of the class. Swaim listened carefully to the questions and issues raised about the story by some members of the class and noted that a small minority had critiqued the work by focusing on what they thought the text should have been rather than what it really was and, as a consequence, the authors felt diminished, marginalised and excluded through the exchange.

Through Swaim's analysis of these two interactions he came to see that the ways in which his students were responding to their peers' writing was not in accord with the intentions underpinning the writing workshops. The students seemed to be having difficulty reacting to the content and intentions of the writing; therefore, there was little motivation for them to write more. In the case of the two students in the peer conference, the use of the language of revision encouraged them to feel as though they had successfully completed the revisionary task so they had little need to do any more. In the case of the class sharing, the authors felt misinterpreted and defensive and so did not see a need to revise their story but rather to seek out a more receptive audience.

As is so common in teacher research, the results of inquiry encourage further inquiry. What Swaim found out about the way in which his students were interacting forced him to look more closely at his teaching. He saw the need to question what he meant by 'honest response and natural connection through writing'. Interestingly, he stumbled across an answer when reading a book primarily written for children, *The Bat-poet* (1964), a story of a bat at odds with other bats but who learns to trust his own instincts and in so doing discovers who he really is. In that story he identified with the reactions of his students to their classmates' writing. The allegorical tale of *The Bat-poet* was a reminder that although social interaction is important in the language-learning process, some kinds of talk are more helpful than others. This is not necessarily a new insight but something he needed to be reminded of, and *The Bat-poet* did that for him.

> I was determined to change my practice and reconstruct writing workshops so that the honest response and natural connection could happen more frequently. In mini-lessons I limited my use of words associated with revision (pruning, expanding, revising, editing, etc.). I was less dogmatic about the purposes of a conference. Children no longer had to meet in pairs. They were encouraged to meet in larger groups and to use it as a time to read their stories out loud and react to them. The job of the author was no longer to come away from the conference with something to change in draft. Instead they were asked only to acknowledge and remember the audience's reaction. Conversely, the job of the audience was to find something in the draft that evoked an emotional response in them and to articulate this reaction as best they could to the author—a tall order for third graders! (Swaim, 1998: 121)

Through this process, Swaim revisited the notion of collaboration and discussed it with his class early in the year. In his mini-lessons, collaboration came to be defined as comprising two important components: small groups (two or three students) working together to compose a story and students being reminded of the need to be more conscious of what their peers were working on in their writing workshops. Each week, students were expected to offer a brief retelling of their work, and through the class sharing sessions ideas could be borrowed by others to assist them in their own writing. An immediate outcome resulting from these changes to the notion of collaboration was that the 'pejorative refrain, "that's copying!", vanished from the class consciousness' (Swaim, 1998: 121). This also meant that students were given time to talk about their writing as they composed it, which Swaim saw as a valuable alternative to rehearsal and planning. However, he was still concerned that the purpose of classroom sharing was not being fully realised. Then, one of his students introduced a story that created a world that included her classmates. This meant that 'the audience was thinking and listening to her story like writers ... not like readers concerned with information and clarity' (Swaim, 1998: 124).

Swaim's teacher research project allowed him to 'listen more intently and read more carefully than ever before' (Swaim, 1998: 124) and allowed him to better identify with the world of his students as writers. He also realised that he had developed a way of teaching about writing that was tied to a view of writing that was not helpful in terms of students' learning about writing: he had been teaching in a way that made it appear as though writing 'was a way of shunting information from one person to the next ... [He was] producing secretaries instead of authors' (Swaim, 1998: 124).

In terms of his professional knowledge of practice he noted that his journey changed his 'theory and practice [of teaching writing], gave [him] new knowledge about the writing process, showed [him] a new metaphor for learning, and offered [him] temporary membership in a fascinating club of writers' (Swaim, 1998: 125). The very nature of that type of knowledge is not something that can really be understood if it is delivered (and interpreted) as 'the right way to teach writing'; it is in fact the type of knowledge that is embedded in personal experience. As a consequence it has a real impact on subsequent practice.

Researching student learning

As a high school mathematics teacher, Pia Jeppesen (2002) always found it frustrating that her students seemed to compartmentalise ideas or methods in their minds, storing them away perhaps for later retrieval but certainly not for making connections from topic to topic, lesson to lesson or between activities. Jeppesen's frustration with her students' apparent lack of linking caused her to want to challenge her students to think more deeply about their role in their learning and to research how that happened, to see if what she did as their teacher really made a difference.

Being familiar with efforts to teach students for enhanced metacognition, she embarked on a teacher research project based on three broad research questions:

- To what extent do specific teaching procedures (for example, thinking books and class discussion) enhance student awareness of the importance of making links and learning strategies involved when making links?

- Does the incidence of linking increase over the time of intervention?

- To what extent do students make links between concepts within a mathematical topic and from topic to topic, and between algorithms within a mathematical topic and from topic to topic?

She did not introduce the project focusing on linking until the second term of the first semester of the school year (each semester has two ten-week terms). However, she did pay careful attention to encouraging students to be respectful of one another and pushed them to begin to think about their learning goals as well as their strengths and weaknesses as learners, which she did through a survey that she called a communication sheet. She taught the set curriculum and, wherever appropriate, did so using teaching procedures designed to encourage metacognition. For example, students selected their own problems; she encouraged students to admit to not understanding;

and she built on students' misconceptions. By the time she was ready to launch into her study on linking (in the second term of semester one), Jeppesen felt confident that her students were comfortable with her approach to teaching and that they were willing to take risks.

> We had established, for example, that all questions were 'good' questions, and no 'put-downs' were allowed, and that homework was usually defined as what each student could achieve in 20 minutes of solid work. The students discovered that I was willing to listen to and use their ideas in the lesson ... and were engaged in their learning and responding positively and constructively to the opportunity to be part of the decision-making process of the lessons. We had also identified experts in various topics within the class who had been able to help their peers. (Jeppesen, 2002: 97–9)

Revisiting the communication sheet, she asked her students to share their personal goals for their learning in maths. This led to discussions about the difference between learning to get something right on a test and learning for understanding.

> Students noted that their good grades on a test or an assignment did not necessarily mean that they could explain concepts and techniques to another person or that they had developed an appropriate understanding of the work ... [they also] indicated a perception that the teacher held all the answers [which] provided an excellent starting point for exploring what the students perceived to be their and my roles in their learning. (Jeppesen, 2002: 99)

Jeppesen then asked her students to complete another communication sheet comprising the beginning of three statements:
- statement 1: Understanding means ...
- statement 2: Learning is about ...
- statement 3: Learning maths is about ...

She collated her students' responses to statements 1 and 2 and constructed two posters: one titled 'Understanding means ...' and another titled 'Learning is about ...' Using these two posters as a stimulus for a brainstorming exercise, the class developed a third poster about how students could work towards achieving a goal of improving their understanding and standard of maths.

Jeppesen continued to teach the set curriculum for the remainder of the year using a wide range of teaching procedures with classroom discussion integral to all lessons. She explicitly promoted student reflection and linking through the use of thinking books (Swan & White, 1994) and two teaching procedures she developed called topic linkup and T-cards. Together, these created a different mathematics classroom teaching and learning environment, which she then set about studying as her teacher research project.

Discussion was crucial for encouraging all members of the class to listen carefully to one another and to establish a forum for the development and refinement of ideas. When Jeppesen thought it was appropriate she would set aside five minutes in class for students to write a paragraph about what they had learned through discussion. These ideas were recorded in their thinking books. Jeppesen believed that private communication at an individual level with students was most important. Thinking books offered a way of doing that and she collected their books on a regular basis in order to follow their thinking and to comment and respond to their ideas.

Topic linkup was a teaching procedure that Jeppesen developed so that students could see the big picture of the whole course and encourage them to make links between topics.

> The headings of each topic to be studied during the year were printed on sixteen blue A4 sheets. These were pinned to the back of the room starting from the first topic in the left hand corner . . . students were generally enthusiastic, adding the links . . . at other times I needed to ask a question such as 'where have you used this type of working before?' I encouraged the students to think about examples and counter examples to support their statements. (Jeppesen, 2002: 103–4)

T-cards (thinking-cards) were developed for recording automatic linking quickly and easily, the purpose being to allow students to practise making links and ensuring that they would not be lost. They also provided a more private way of recording ideas—they noted the date, the topic and the link on their card. Students could write on their cards at any time throughout a lesson and were encouraged to share their thoughts with a neighbour or the rest of the class. 'Often I would ask for "T-card links" as part of the general discussion at the end of the lesson. On occasion, I would provide a few minutes in class for students to privately record any links which had been made during a lesson. This would be followed by voluntary discussion. I also encouraged the students to use them during homework time.' (Jeppesen, 2002: 104)

Over the course of the year Jeppesen found that students became more confident learners and more aware of the nature of high quality learning. They also became much more comfortable at sharing ideas and felt 'secure in the knowledge that they would be taken seriously and their ideas would be valued' (Jeppesen, 2002: 104).

At the end of term 3 (halfway through the second semester of the school year) she asked students to complete another communication sheet based on ideas and linking and the activities they had been using to promote linking. Her analysis of their responses showed her that the students had 'developed a sense of the network of links between different topics . . . [and their] awareness of the big picture . . . [but] were ambivalent about the use of thinking books' (Jeppesen, 2002: 106). She also found that the students who were more confident in maths tended to be more comfortable and capable in being part of the decision-making processes in the class.

There was an interesting aspect to this study that surprised Jeppesen and her students. Halfway through term 4 the students told her that they were overloaded by all the thinking and the talk associated with the way the maths classes were being conducted. So together they agreed to a lesson based on a more traditional approach. However, the students didn't like the lesson because they became passive observers. They found themselves bored and uninterested in the lesson and actually asked her to stop teaching that way and to allow them to ask questions and raise issues themselves. They told her: 'We like being able to work things out for ourselves. We want to ask you for help when we need it. [We] want to try to make up some really hard questions' (Jeppesen, 2002: 111).

At the end of the year the students were given the communication sheet they had completed in the first lesson. They reflected on what they had written and then responded anew. Jeppesen's analysis of these sheets showed that there had been a change in her students' attitudes and perceptions about their performance. She felt as though they had come to recognise in themselves the growth in their confidence and their ability as learners as well as their role in influencing the direction of a lesson or topic. Seventy-five per cent of those that responded through their communication sheets believed they were better maths learners as a result of the way they had been taught and the way they had approached learning during the year. The study also had important implications for the way Jeppesen thought about her teaching:

> This study added a new dimension to the way in which I reflected on and approached my teaching. It meant that, in addition to thinking about the issues of learning associated with each topic, I formally reflected on a particular aspect of quality learning (linking) as well as the overall direction of the whole year. The shift in my focus directly impacted on how the students responded to my teaching and thus on their reflection on their learning. The main differences between this class and classes that I had taught in previous years with a general focus of teaching for quality learning were:
>
> - I was better able to harness and maintain interest levels of the students;
> - stronger teacher–student rapport;
> - more stable class dynamics, with all students feeling comfortable with taking risks; and
> - I was more systematic and purposeful in promoting quality learning and more students displayed characteristics of independent learning.
>
> This study has clearly shown me that students can be mature and confident thinkers and learners and teachers do students a disservice if they do not provide opportunities for them to be responsible for taking a major part in their own learning. (Jeppesen, 2002: 113)

Overview

This chapter was designed to draw attention to the work of teacher researchers and to highlight the importance and value of such work in shaping understandings of the professional knowledge of practice. Although teacher research is usually an additional task on top of the already demanding work of teaching, there are important questions about teaching and learning that can only be developed and examined in classrooms by teachers. Teacher research generates specialist knowledge that is immediately applicable and meaningful for practice and that is a most important research outcome. Teacher research offers real possibilities for demonstrating the type of evidence that teachers can readily identify with in supporting their efforts for enhancing quality in teaching and learning.

12

Developing knowledge of practice through professional learning

In recent times there has been a shift in the language associated with teacher development. The notion of professional learning has slowly crept in to the literature. That which used to be described as professional development is now often termed professional learning. However, the replacement of one term with another is not helpful because it undermines the difference in meaning that the language is supposed to imply.

Professional development has typically been understood as the more traditional approach to in-service that teachers often experience when they are asked to implement a new curriculum or some other policy initiative. In many cases, the waves of change that regularly flow over the profession generally involve some form of up-skilling in relation to the new things that we are expected to do or to deliver. Therefore, traditional professional development is often linked to the implementation of some form of educational change by doing something *to* teachers, that is, telling us about the change and expecting it to then be carried out. In this way, mandated changes are presented, we are trained in those changes in terms of technical requirements (sometimes as simple as re-labelling existing curriculum and practice) and then we are expected to implement those changes. It is a top-down approach and it functions in a similar way throughout the education system whether it be in the form of policy initiatives from the central education bureaucracy or at local school level from the principal's office. Professional development in that sense is then about making changes that have been formed elsewhere but henceforth need to be implemented in classrooms.

Professional learning operates in a different way. Professional learning assumes that we have some commitment to the change(s)—that the change might be driven, or developed and refined, by us. In essence, professional learning works on the basis that change is as a result of work *with*, and/or *by*, teachers. Further to this, professional learning also carries an expectation that we are able to bring our expert judgement to bear on how change might best be implemented in our own context and practice. Therefore, professional learning is more about the learning that occurs through the process and how that learning is then able to be applied in our practice. Involvement in professional learning is therefore more likely to be voluntary, and the subsequent learning is personal and appropriately shaped and directed by each of us as individuals.

Refining practice

The need for activities that work reflects how important it is for us to be continually expanding and developing the range of teaching procedures we have at hand for engaging our students in learning. However, there is a difference between gathering an armoury of teaching procedures and being able to use them appropriately. Moving beyond doing activities that work and purposefully developing knowledge of why those activities work is the type of learning about practice that can't be mandated by others.

In a project developed with a group of teachers from a number of different schools (Lancaster et al., 2007), the teachers involved focused on the decisions they made and the actions they took to support and encourage their students' need to know in learning science. They shared their work by writing blogs based on a number of different topics. One topic in particular was student questioning. Although student questioning sounds quite straightforward, it is interesting how their inquiries led to a range of outcomes that would not have been so likely had they not been directing the work in ways appropriate to their learning about their practice. Through this topic of student questioning a number of themes emerged, as explained below.

Withholding judgement

Despite the planning that goes into preparing lessons, the immediacy of the classroom places demands on teachers as we are continually called upon to make judgements about aspects of our practice and how the decisions we make influence students' learning. Our natural tendency is to maintain an appropriate flow of ideas and actions designed to help our students further their understanding of the content being examined. In teaching there is a strong sense of a need to continually be moving on, to be building momentum and creating challenges that will lead students to be engaged in learning.

At first glimpse, then, it could appear somewhat paradoxical to suggest that *withholding judgement* might be helpful in fostering student engagement. However, its purpose is related to creating a space for student thinking and decision-making so that we are not necessarily directing them in terms of what to learn, but giving them opportunities to make choices about their learning; such possibilities are severely diminished if our students feel as though we are making judgements about their ideas, thoughts and actions. Therefore, it is important to pay careful attention to the notion of withholding judgement because, in many ways, it is about slowing down the natural tendency to make quick assessments when responding to students. Similarly, students can be invited to consider more possibilities and make alternative suggestions and offer different ideas in the way they engage with the subject matter.

The point of withholding judgement is to create divergent responses to situations so that open-ended inquiry might be encouraged (as opposed to slowing the pace in order to increase student understanding while aiming for the right answer or correct solution). It then might be demonstrated in a range of teacher behaviours and be encouraged through varied teaching procedures. The important point here is that if we concentrate on withholding judgement, students are given real choices about the way in which their thinking might be developed and tested in their learning. For example, consider the following blog entry by Bree Moody.

Letting kids experiment

Early in the term, the kids started asking some really good questions (particularly during experiments). The questions were often right off the topic and often related to the application of concepts. These questions frightened me. I didn't always know the answer or how to explain them. Often they were highlighting the limitations of scientific models.

Instead of giving them a straightforward answer, or brushing off their ideas, I encouraged them to discuss, hypothesise and experiment to find answers to their questions.

Example:

Question: 'When wood is burning, is the smoke evaporated wood?'
Student solution: He grabbed some wood shavings, set them alight and placed a beaker over the top to catch some smoke. He then asked for some ice, which he placed on the beaker to try and condense the smoke. To show/see if wood would reappear? He noticed some water vapour appear and floating black ash.

This led to many more questions and hypotheses.

What I learnt:
• Often this was risky. Kids were all doing different experiments and coming up with theories that I knew were totally incorrect.
• Kids were more than capable of developing novel techniques. Often their ideas were better than the ones I could think of.
• Some kids struggled to think up ideas independently, and required guidance in thinking about what test to employ.
• I had to make sure I didn't give away answers and allow the students the time & freedom needed to properly explore their ideas. (quoted in Lancaster et al., 2007)

Here Moody demonstrates what it means to withhold judgement. Her natural inclination would no doubt have been to tell the student the answer to his question. For some of us, it would perhaps have been difficult not to do so inadvertently by commenting on the logic of the question itself. However, this blog entry illustrates that Moody must have been quite thoughtful and conscious of her skills in this area because, in many ways, the very question the student asked may not have been so readily and openly raised in some other science classrooms.

As Moody notes, in withholding judgement she invites students' questions, which can be quite challenging; especially so when she does not know the answers herself. We have all experienced this kind of pressure and how the responses we may have developed can invite or close down further discussion or inquiry. But by creating the possibilities for students' questions to arise, the content underpinning those questions is able to be focused on in ways that might lead to the development of deeper conceptual understandings.

Although the blog entry makes it appear that withholding judgement is a natural part of her practice, it is not quite so simple. Moody shows how she holds back in such a way as to encourage her students to use their developing understanding of the content as a source of engagement rather than being directed by the teacher. By encouraging and inviting students' questions, the classroom becomes a more collaborative environment in which students can develop a greater sense of ownership over what is being learned; this sense of shared intellectual control is a vital component of student interest.

An obvious and immediate benefit for the teacher is that students' questions may also bring to the surface alternative conceptions—of which the teacher may or may not be aware. Alternative conceptions that you might expect can be helpful feedback on the way the teaching and learning is unfolding; alternative conceptions of which you are unaware may create new possibilities for further inquiry into the peculiarities or difficulties of the content.

Withholding judgement, then, may at the simplest level be initiated by not judging students' comments, questions and ideas, while at a more sophisticated level it might involve the ability to maintain openness to students' responses and a purposeful agenda for creating and inviting such behaviours in student learning on a regular basis. In many ways, it requires a teacher to be prepared to take risks in their teaching.

Risk taking

Withholding judgement and encouraging students to question content can indeed be challenging and could be viewed by some as highlighting a teaching weakness. However, although withholding judgement is an important teaching behaviour, it is the learning that prevails that is the real focus of attention rather than the teaching per se. Moody's blog entry highlights some of the risks associated with the consequences of her withholding judgement in terms of her entry about what she learnt.

It requires a great deal of confidence to risk allowing students to work on different experiments at the same time and it would clearly be challenging to withhold judgement in the hope that through designing experiments students will arrive at the correct theory. Another aspect of risk in withholding judgement is in relation to what Moody describes as *student independence* or their *level of required guidance*. In allowing for these differences, the normal expectation that the class moves forward together, preferably at the same pace towards a particular content destination, brings into sharp focus the real contradiction of such a view in light of the reality of diverse learning styles and varied ability within all classrooms. Recognising the problem therefore invites a pedagogical response.

Finally, in being conscious of the purpose of withholding judgement, Moody also recognised the risks associated with what could happen if she reverted to type and the impact that could have on her students' learning: 'I had to make sure I didn't give away answers'. If she did, her invitations and expectations for her students to be engaged would serve little purpose because 'the time and freedom needed to properly explore their ideas' would not be forthcoming. The genuineness inherent in how you withhold judgement is therefore crucial to the way in which learning outcomes might be recognised and taken up on a more regular basis. It is as much about an expectation as a practice; the more each reflects the other, the more likely the invitation will be seen by students as real. The more real it is, the more likely they will give of themselves as learners.

Open-mindedness

As noted in Chapter 10, early last century John Dewey outlined an argument about the nature and importance of reflection. His definition involved two central features: '(1) a state of doubt, hesitation, perplexity, mental difficulty, in which thinking originates, and (2) an act of searching, hunting, inquiring, to find material that will resolve the doubt, settle and dispose of the perplexity' (Dewey, 1933: 12). It is not difficult, then, to see how important reflective thinking is for engaging students in their learning; they need to be given choices and they need to exercise decision-making. Dewey also described attitudes that matter in underpinning reflective thinking, one of which is *open-mindedness*. As the term suggests, open-mindedness depends on an ability to consider problems in new and different ways, to be open to new ideas and thoughts that one may not have previously entertained. To be open-minded is to be ready to listen to more sides than one, to be an active listener, to be prepared and able to hear thinking that may be contrary to one's own and to be able to admit that a previously held belief may in fact be wrong (Loughran, 1996: 4–5).

It is not so difficult to be open-minded when considering new ideas, curious or compelling problems or interesting situations that do not necessarily carry personal consequences. It is much harder to be open-minded when one is comfortable with a particular view or approach to doing things, or when alternative or opposing views are personally confronting or challenging. Being open-minded is something that both teachers and students need to actively develop if choices in teaching and learning are to be seriously considered.

Despite how she might have felt about her teaching and her students' learning, in the way she responded to her students' inquiries Moody illustrated that she was very open-minded. She noted a sense of reluctance about being asked questions that she could not answer yet her actions encouraged her to be placed in that very situation. In being open to possibilities that she may not have previously considered, which challenged her normal teaching approach, she created real possibilities for her students to be engaged in their science learning because they were able to approach the problems they had arrived at with an open mind. If she had told her student that smoke was not evaporated wood, he may not have taken the opportunity to reflect on the problem and attempt to solve it himself, and therefore may not have been engaged in his science learning to anywhere near the extent that was illustrated in her blog entry.

Just as Moody's ability to be open-minded was important in terms of how she responded in the moment through her teaching, so too her students were given opportunities to be open-minded in the way in which they could then examine the problems that they had chosen to tackle. Thinking about this aspect of Moody's experimentation with her practice suggests that perhaps the notion of open-mindedness might be better, or more fruitfully, enacted in learning if the attitude and the way it impacts learning were made more explicit through our practice and highlighted in the advantages for students' learning. However, to be open-minded is one thing, and to be able to respond to the possibilities for enacting it in practice is another; it requires a certain level of independence.

Independence

For decision-making and choice to be real for students, there is an obvious need for their independence to be encouraged. Success in school learning is often traditionally viewed by students (and perhaps by teachers as well) as being linked to things such as guessing what's in the teacher's head or being able to reproduce the right information in the right way on tests or other forms of assessment. But success could also be viewed in terms of such things as posing questions that are publicly valued and used by teachers or finding alternative ways to address a problem or situation. The difference between these two perspectives is that the encouragement of the latter requires a certain level of student independence in terms of choices and decisions in thinking and action, as illustrated through the following blog entry by Vojtech Markus.

Letting the students decide the content

Having established a pretty good learning environment with my Year 9 class over the course of the year, I decided to take a large risk with my approach to teaching and challenge the students in a way that I have never attempted before. Over a four-week period prior to exams they were going to have to come to class and decide what they were going to learn within the context of photosynthesis and cell respiration. This would involve the class deciding the content to be covered, the context, the practical experiments to be attempted and what my role would be in explaining content within the topic.

This initial comment was met with a few concerned faces among the students. I could see there was going to be a need for a fair bit of clarification and support (something I was expecting anyway). I tried to comfort them by emphasising that all of us (including me) were on a journey together and that my role over the next four weeks was to assist them on their journey.

Each student received a Student Booklet that was intended to be their guide through this unit as well as a record of the work they had completed. The booklet broke up the unit into six smaller sub-units. Each sub-unit referred to a relevant section of a textbook or a particular hand-out. There were also a series of tasks that needed to be completed, as well as a few expert tasks. On top of that the booklet also contained their assessment for the unit which comprised six tasks based on Bloom's Taxonomy (Remember, Understand, Analyse, Evaluate, Create, etc.). (Lancaster et al., 2007)

Markus's approach would most certainly result in students focusing on a range of different content within the topic, but how they might then do the task depended on them genuinely being able to make decisions about what to do, how and why. If they were not independent, they would simply be following a recipe. Markus describes his reasons for trialling this approach to student research: 'The big picture side of the topic is one that I feel might be better captured by the students if they have tried to discover the links between content by themselves first.' Beyond his need to provide some initial guidance to his students, allowing them to decide the content they would learn required handing over responsibility for learning in ways that many of us could find difficult to implement in our own classrooms. There is a real possibility that students might be overwhelmed by the broad range of content available and therefore not be able to prioritise its importance or value. Yet the independence necessary to make decisions about those choices is at the heart of being engaged in the learning in ways that go beyond guessing what's in the teacher's head or embarking on the search for the right answer in the right way. It also says a lot about how professional learning is tied to the type of risk a teacher is comfortable in taking.

In considering the ways in which withholding judgement might be enacted in teaching and learning situations, it is not difficult to see how, through Moody and Markus's explorations of their students' learning, they were creating situations for their own professional learning. Some of the knowledge they developed is encapsulated in the themes of risk taking, open-mindedness and independence briefly considered above. However, that knowledge is not described in terms of generalised rules that then govern everything they do. Rather, their knowledge is about the way their teaching intent is carried out and translated into student learning. Their professional learning as a consequence of directing their own inquiries led them to know new things about student engagement that might not have emerged, or been acted on, if they had not been in control of what they were doing, how and why. They clearly developed their expertise as professionals and, as a consequence, learnt more about the nature of pedagogy.

Accepting responsibility for developing and directing our own professional learning is an important aspect of teaching.

Learning about the knowledge of practice

In his compelling account of teaching a Year 7 class, when reviewing his experiences at the end of the year Jeff Northfield was struck by the fact that his:

> wide understanding of educational theories did not seem to assist [him] in interpreting many of the situations which arose in the classroom. There seemed to be few guidelines for future actions . . . In the end, the unique classroom situations require unique and creative responses by teachers which are based on many considerations. (Loughran & Northfield, 1996: 138)

As he reflected on his experiences, what he did, how and why, Northfield mused over the ways in which the day-to-day teaching experience led him to think about his knowledge of practice. He described how there was little time or opportunity to explicitly share or disseminate his knowledge and so it remained largely tacit. He also began to see how his knowledge was personal and unique to particular classroom contexts, and that even among his colleagues knowledge of practice was not viewed as particularly significant— partly because it is context specific and not generalisable.

In reflecting on his experiences, Northfield came to understand more about his knowledge of practice and how important it was to find ways of sharing the learning from critical classroom experiences with others so that the tacit became explicit. In that way, the knowledge underpinning experience can be evaluated and reviewed so that the assumptions underpinning practice can be questioned and alternative frames considered.

One outcome of that process was most striking in his analysis of his efforts. He described situations in which his teaching intentions were at odds with his students' school-learning expectations. As a result, teaching and learning did not always exist in a reciprocal relationship. Rather, they tended to be pulling in opposite directions. He described these differences through two different views of teaching and learning: his teacher view and his students' view (Loughran & Northfield, 1996: 137). See Table 12.1 for a summary of these two views.

As a consequence of juxtaposing these alternative frames of teaching and learning, Northfield saw something different that was not so obvious to him when he was embroiled in the day-to-day demands of teaching. He saw that the value of active learning, thinking and understanding was not so evident to his students and so his teaching agenda was not appreciated by them in ways that allowed his pedagogical intentions to be fully realised. However, by listening carefully to his students he found ways of capitalising on opportunities as they arose, but he was surprised at how often those situations were unplanned. His experience reinforced why pedagogical expertise, by the very nature of the individuality and isolation of classroom practice, remained tacit and often misunderstood, even by teachers themselves.

The ability to explicate knowledge of practice is therefore clearly dependent on creating time and space for reflection, sharing and critique. This is a common theme evident throughout the literature but it rarely seems to be acted on in any formal way by education

Table 12.1 Teacher and student views of teaching and learning

A personal/teacher view of teaching and learning	Some student views of teaching and learning
Where possible students should have opportunities to be active and think about their learning experiences.	Learning is associated with gaining right answers, and thinking and personal understanding are just different and often frustrating ways of achieving the required outcomes.
Students should experience success in learning and gain confidence and skills to become better learners.	The learning process and thinking is difficult to associate with school work, and texts and notes are important indicators that school learning is occurring.
Linking experiences from both within and outside school greatly assist learning.	Linking experiences is very demanding and unreasonable when added to the classroom demands for students.
Effort and involvement are important outcomes of school activities and students need to gain credit and encouragement for their efforts.	The final grade is the critical outcome and the basis by which progress is judged.
Enjoyment and satisfaction with learning are important outcomes.	Enjoyment is not always associated with school learning—real learning is hard and not usually enjoyed.
Learning involving the above features requires learner consent.	Learning is done to students, and teachers have a major responsibility for achieving learning.

Source: Loughran & Northfield, 1996

authorities. In order to create real opportunities for professional learning, there is a need for teaching to be understood as comprising much more than just the doing of teaching. Professional learning leads to enhanced pedagogical expertise and therefore improves the quality of student learning.

As Amanda Berry described in her extensive study of her teaching (Berry, 2007), by focusing on her teaching and her students' learning, in developing an evidence base on which she could make informed conclusions, a number of key issues about practice emerged for her that dramatically shaped her professional learning. Her knowledge of practice was developed around a range of major themes: framing and reframing; distinguishing between technical aspects of practice and understanding practice; trusting students as learners; developing self-understanding and awareness; and the value of collaboration. All of these themes have much to say about knowledge of practice and its importance in shaping our understandings of pedagogy.

Framing and reframing

The busyness of teaching encourages framing of situations in particular ways. For example, we have all experienced the curriculum pressure associated with completing the syllabus in time, or the assessment pressure created by requirements of testing and evaluation. These situations frame how we prioritise what we do and how we think about progress. In some instances, this framing can encourage a stronger concentration on content over understanding and make it difficult to see other ways of acting. Reframing is when the same situation is viewed from alternative perspectives so that different ways of acting are more readily apparent. In responding to alternative perspectives new knowledge of practice emerges. What that knowledge is and how it influences teaching and learning will vary from teacher to teacher. Some outcomes will encourage further experimentation with pedagogy; others will reinforce existing views. Therefore, although the outcomes of professional learning might not be able to be stated in absolute terms, that does not limit the value of the process itself. Seeking to see beyond existing frames of practice is one way of enhancing the professional knowledge of practice.

Understanding teaching beyond the technical

Teaching requires technical proficiency. However, moving beyond the technical is crucial for the development of pedagogical expertise. When attempting to implement a new teaching procedure, particular aspects of using that procedure need to be mastered and so the skills in using that procedure must be developed. In concentrating on getting the procedure to work, the technical matters. For example, it is hard to run a jigsaw group-work activity if groups are not evenly divided to begin with or if the number of students in a group does not correspond to the number of questions or activities set for completion. But, once familiarity with the procedure has been established, the real impact on the quality of the teaching and learning occurs when the expert pedagogue adjusts, adapts and innovates using that procedure in response to the professional judgements made about its use in that teacher's particular context. Again, what that means in terms of the knowledge developed varies from teacher to teacher and context to context. In some instances it might mean that the teaching procedure proves to be particularly helpful with specific content and so our pedagogical content knowledge may be enhanced. In other instances it might mean that the purpose for using the procedure (for example, as a diagnostic tool, or to preview or review a unit of work) becomes clearer as a result of developing a deeper understanding of its value at a particular time during a unit of work. It is in situations such as these that expertise is developed because the problematic nature of teaching invites exploration and so teaching operates as an educative rather than rudimentary training process.

Trusting students as learners

Research over the years has illustrated how important it is to us that the effort we put into teaching is translated into positive learning outcomes for our students. It is hard to imagine how any teacher could not have the best interests of their students at heart. In fact, for many, it is this sense of commitment to others that underpins their career. This sense of responsibility plays out in many different ways in teaching. In some cases, we subconsciously direct and control classrooms in ways that encourage students to be passive and dependent learners. Because we want our students to learn our subject 'the right way' we leave little room for students to manoeuvre in terms of accepting responsibility for their own learning. A difficult aspect of teaching is being able to create ways of working that build the capacity and motivation of students to take responsibility for learning and to direct meaning making so that learning extends beyond acquiring the information alone. Professional learning opportunities that allow us to confidently construct pedagogy in ways that facilitate students as active learners have a major role in developing professional knowledge of practice. Considerably more expertise is required when we genuinely support our students as active learners in contrast to giving them directed activities that simply facilitate the transfer of knowledge and information. Teaching for understanding is more complex and demanding than teaching as telling, and the professional knowledge that underpins such practice, is special and should be valued and highly prized.

Self-understanding and awareness

Amanda Berry notes that 'developing my self-understanding and self-awareness is prerequisite to helping others see themselves in ways that enable them to help themselves [as learners]' (Berry, 2007: 163). This is an important point because although we may not immediately recognise it, we often teach in ways similar to the way we were taught. The things we didn't like as students we sometimes inadvertently do as teachers. Berry reminds us of the importance of knowing who we are and how we operate so that we can critically appraise our work in ways that might encourage our pedagogical development to incorporate the learning of those who learn in ways other than those with which we are familiar and comfortable and in so doing, teach in ways that might be supportive of those different learning approaches.

Jack Whitehead (1993) described the uncomfortable times he experienced in his teaching when he did things that were not in accord with his intentions—he recognised that his practices and beliefs clashed. He described those moments in which he felt that way as being a 'living contradiction'. We all have experienced this. The real issue is what we do about it. The typical response is to gloss over or ignore such moments. It is easy to rationalise our behaviour. But in doing so we begin to reinforce those behaviours, and so those moments of feeling like a living contradiction become embedded in the way we teach—and so are even more difficult to recognise and react to in meaningful ways. Whitehead, like Berry, did not ignore or gloss over these moments. Both chose to think more carefully about what such instances meant for their practice and their students' learning. Both thought about who they were and how they acted and how their views translated into actions in practice. As a consequence, both were able to see themselves from different perspectives (students' perspectives in particular). By being more aware of their own behaviours, Whitehead and Berry were more able to align their teaching intentions with their teaching actions. They developed substantial understanding about themselves as teachers and that is a central component to knowledge of practice—who we are is an integral element of how we teach. Self-understanding and self-awareness inform our professional knowledge of practice.

Collaboration

Teaching, like few other jobs, demands a lot from us because of the sustained contact with others and the obvious heavy reliance on good interpersonal skills necessary for ongoing success. Working with a diversity of students lesson after lesson can be taxing as each has different needs, concerns and expectations of us as teachers, and of themselves as learners. We have to manage these variations in order to ensure that our students individually, and as a group, maintain a positive and open attitude towards learning.

Typically, schooling structures revolve around a group of students with one teacher. Therefore, somewhat paradoxically, once we close the classroom door we are alone and professionally isolated and that professional isolation can be difficult to break down. Collaboration in teaching can occur in many ways, but central to learning through collaboration for the development of professional knowledge of practice is the value of planning, teaching and reviewing practice with a valued colleague. Amanda Berry describes how her learning through collaboration helped her to challenge the:

> taken-for-granted assumptions [because] through shared experiences I was able to gain a range of perspectives . . . and develop greater meaning from these experiences because they were shared . . . [collaboration] forced me to confront some of my assumptions about practice [and] support the personal demands associated with self-study research since a shared experience can be made much more personally manageable than when that experience is borne alone . . . I can see that [I have made] concrete shifts in practice as well as conceptual shifts in understanding. (Berry, 2007: 164–5)

Collaboration with a trusted colleague can create situations through which many aspects of practice can be reconsidered through open and honest reflection. It is sometimes too easy to be defensive of our actions or to rationalise and justify our behaviours. Collaboration can help to break down those barriers and encourage learning about what we do, how and why. Through that process we are more likely to be open to recognise and respond appropriately to the problematic nature of teaching.

Overview

This chapter outlined the distinction between professional development and professional learning in order to highlight a number of important issues that matter for the growth and valuing of teachers' professional knowledge of practice. Through a serious focus on professional learning, what we know and are able to do as teachers takes on new significance when understood in terms of professional autonomy and judgement. The nature of professional learning is inevitably personal and idiosyncratic as we make sense of the ways in which big-picture teaching and learning issues are able to be translated in our own context and practice. It is through the personal understanding that is developed as a result of carefully examining teaching and learning that teachers' professional knowledge of practice grows and pedagogical expertise is developed and refined. Through the examples of teachers' work offered in this chapter, the essence of professional learning has been portrayed in ways that have been designed to demonstrate why it is so important that we direct and control our own professional learning.

13
Conclusion

In order to move beyond teaching as telling there is a need to understand the problematic nature of practice. In so doing, teaching immediately stands out as demanding and highly complex. Although expert teachers may make teaching look easy, the reality is that it requires specialist skills, knowledge and ability. However, making those things clear for others to see and understand is no simple task.

> *Teaching is unforgivingly complex.* It is not simply good or bad, right or wrong, working or failing. Although absolutes and dichotomies such as these are popular in the headlines . . . they are limited in their usefulness. They tacitly assume there is consensus across our diverse society about the purposes of schooling and what it means to be engaged in the process of becoming an educated person as well as consensus about whose knowledge and values are of most worth and what counts as evidence of the effectiveness of teaching and learning. They ignore almost completely the nuances of 'good' (or 'bad') teaching of real students collected in actual classrooms in the context of particular times and places . . . measures of this work cannot be determined by narrow conceptions of teaching quality and student learning that focus exclusively on test scores and ignore the incredible complexity of teaching and learning and its institutional realities inherent in the accountability context. (Cochran-Smith, 2003: 4)

Teaching is a highly public profession. Because schooling has been such an integral component of most people's formative years, there is a sense of familiarity with what teaching looks like and how it is done. To many, it appears that teaching involves packaging up knowledge and information and then imparting it to a group of students. From this perspective, a good teacher is one who delivers information with some humour or other interesting personal style that makes absorbing that information a bit more enjoyable or even fun. However, this view of teaching ignores the complexity of the interaction between teaching and learning. Most of this complexity is not immediately apparent to observers of teaching because they do not hear what the teacher is thinking or do not recognise the way a teacher's experience influences what they know about how to best do their job.

Seeing the complexity in teaching can be difficult because the crucial link to learning can be overlooked or learning may be confused with absorbing information. Sadly, if learning is seen as simply absorbing information, it reinforces the view that teaching is made up of clever tricks and routines that make information easy to remember. Therefore, teaching can be confused with telling and retelling information—even if it is done in interesting ways. However, if learning is understood as comprising such things as building on existing knowledge, creating links to related ideas, processing information and reorganising and synthesising that knowledge, and developing students' metacognitive skills, then teaching as telling will not suffice.

The quality of teaching is evident in the teacher's sensitivity to students' learning. But because students do not all learn in the same way, high quality teaching demands responsiveness to different learning styles and approaches. In so doing, it becomes obvious that in order to be sensitive and responsive to learners' needs, teaching is no simple task; it is indeed complex. That complexity increases when a consideration of content is included.

Expertise in teaching begins to strongly stand out when teachers shape their practice in particular ways that they know make a difference for their students' learning of particular subject content, which contrasts dramatically to a teaching–as–telling perspective. Teaching as telling might involve repeating the same information over and over again until it sinks in, saying it more loudly, or writing it down for students to copy and hopefully absorb. Pedagogical expertise involves (among other things) creating ways for students to manipulate the important ideas of the subject; to think about how to use that content in similar and different situations; and to recognise and respond to issues and ideas that they find personally difficult to understand. Teaching is clearly complex when meaningful learning is the goal. It is of course much easier to deliver information than purposefully develop learners' engagement with content. It is much easier to measure retention of information as opposed to assess meaningful understanding. It is also much easier to offer solutions to teaching problems if teaching itself is seen as uncomplicated and straightforward. But teaching isn't simple and straightforward; teaching is complex.

As teachers we should be able to demonstrate and articulate that which comprises our expertise. We need to be able to make our skills, abilities and knowledge of pedagogy clear and obvious. In so doing, we highlight the importance of our specialist knowledge of practice, firstly for ourselves, but also for others. Through such a process it is immediately obvious what teaching really involves and so it is more likely that new and more informed ways of understanding might prevail.

Bibliography

Baird, J. R. (1986a) Improving learning through enhanced metacognition: A classroom study, *European Journal of Science Education*, 8, 263–82.

——(1986b) Learning and teaching: The need for change, in J. R. Baird & I. J. Mitchell (Eds) *Improving the quality of teaching and learning: An Australian case study—The PEEL project* (pp. 6–13), Melbourne: Monash University Print Services.

Baird, J. R. & Mitchell, I. J. (Eds) (1986) *Improving the quality of teaching and learning: An Australian case study—The PEEL project*, Melbourne: Monash University Print Services.

Baird, J. R. & Northfield, J. R. (Eds) (1992) *Learning from the PEEL experience*, Melbourne: Monash University Print Services.

Berry, A. (2004) Self-study in teaching about teaching, in J. Loughran, M. L. Hamilton, V. LaBoskey & T. Russell (Eds) *International handbook of self-study of teaching and teacher education practices* (vol. 2, pp. 1295–332), Dordrecht: Kluwer.

——(2007) *Tensions in teaching about teaching: Understanding practice as a teacher educator*, Dordrecht: Springer.

Berry, A. & Milroy, P. (2002) Changes that matter, in J. Loughran, I. Mitchell & J. Mitchell (Eds), *Learning from teacher research* (pp. 196–221), New York: Teachers College Press.

Biggs, J. B. (1999) What the student does: Teaching for enhanced student learning, *Higher Education Research & Development*, 18(1), (pp. 57–75).

Birbili, M. (2006) Mapping Knowledge: Concept maps in early childhood education, *Early Childhood Research & Practice (ECRP)*, vol. 8, no. 2, online journal available at <www.ecrp.uiuc.edu/v8n2/birbili.html>.

Bloom, B. S. (Ed.) (1956) *Taxonomy of educational objectives: Handbook 1. Cognitive domain*, New York: Longman, Green.

Boyle, L. (2002) Disasters and metacognition in the SOSE classroom, in J. Loughran, I. Mitchell & J. Mitchell (Eds) *Learning from teacher research* (pp. 74–88), New York: Teachers College Press.

Brookfield, S. D. (1995) *Becoming a critically reflective teacher*, San Francisco. Jossey-Bass Publishers.

Buehl, D. (2001) *Classroom strategies to interactive learning*, Newark, NJ: International Reading Association.

Buzan, T. (2002) *How to mind map*, London: Thorsons.

Calderhead, J. (1988) The development of knowledge structures in learning to teach, in J. Calderhead (Ed.), *Teachers' professional learning* (pp. 51–64), London: Falmer Press.

Cochran-Smith, M. (2003) The unforgiving complexity of teaching: Avoiding simplicity in the age of accountability, *Journal of Teacher Education*, 54(1), (pp. 3–5).

Cochran-Smith, M., & Lytle, S. (1999) Relationships of knowledge and practice: Teacher learning communities, in A. Iran-Nejad & P. D. Pearson (Eds) *Review of Research in Education* (vol. 24, pp. 249–305), Washington DC: American Educational Research Association.

——(2004) Practitioner inquiry, knowledge, and university culture, in J. J. Loughran, M. L. Hamilton, V. K. LaBoskey & T. Russell (Eds) *International handbook of self-study of teaching and teacher education practices* (vol. 1, pp. 601–49), Dordrecht: Kluwer Academic Press.

DeBono, E. (1992) *Six thinking hats for school*, Cheltenham: HawkerBrownlow.

Dewey, J. (1929) *The sources for a science of education*, New York: Liveright.

——(1933) *How we think*, Lexington, MA: D. C. Heath and Company.

——(Ed.) (1964) *John Dewey on education: Selected writings*, Chicago: University of Chicago Press.

Dochy, F. (1992) *Assessment of prior knowledge as the determinant of future learning*, Utrecht, London: Lemma BV/Kingsley Publishers.

Dochy, F., Segers, M. & Buehl, M. (1999) The relation between assessment practices and outcomes of studies: The case of research on prior knowledge, *Review of Educational Research*, 69(2), (pp. 145–86).

English Heritage (2007) 'Teachers Notes: Victorian buildings card sort', *Victorian Buildings: Victorian Minds*, National Monuments Record, Heritage Explorer, <www.heritageexplorer.org.uk/web/he/searchdetail.aspx?id=1203&crit=victorian>.

Fagan, E., Hassler, D., & Szabo, M. (1981) Evaluation of questioning strategies in language arts instruction, *Research in the Teaching of English*, 15, (pp. 267–73).

Fenstermacher, G. D. (1994) The knower and the known: The nature of knowledge in research on teaching, in L. Darling-Hammond (Ed.) *Review of Research in Education* (vol. 20, pp. 3–56), Washington DC: American Educational Research Association.

Flavell, J. H. (1976) Metacognitive aspects of problem-solving, in L. B. Resnick (Ed.) *Nature of intelligence*, Hillsdale, NJ: Erlbaum.

Freire, P. (1972) *Pedagogy of the oppressed*, New York: Herder & Herder.

Freire, P. & Macedo, D. (1995) A dialogue: Culture, language, and race, *Harvard Educational Review*, 65(3), (pp. 379–402).

Gardner, H. (1983) *Frames of mind: The theory of multiple intelligences*, New York: Basic Books.

Goleman, D. (1996) *Emotional intelligence: Why it can matter more than IQ*, London: Bloomsbury.

Gordon, W. J. J. (1961) *Synectics: The development of creative capacity*, New York: Harper.

Grant, P., Johnson, L. & Sanders, Y. (1990) *Better links: Teaching strategies in science class*, Parkville, Melbourne: STAV Publishing.

Grimmett, P. P. & MacKinnon, A. M. (1992) Craft knowledge and the education of teachers, in G. Grant (Ed.) *Review of Research in Education* (vol. 18, pp. 385–456), Washington DC: American Educational Research Association.

Higher Education Academy (2008) Deep and surface approaches to learning, retrieved 14 November 2008, <www.engsc.ac.uk/er/theory/learning.asp>.

Hoban, G. (2005) From claymation to slowmation: A teaching procedure to develop students' science understandings, *Australian Science Teachers Journal*, 51(2), (pp. 26–30).

Houghton, W. (2004) *Engineering Subject Centre Guide: Learning and Teaching Theory for Engineering Academics*, Loughborough: Higher Education Academy Engineering Subject Centre, available online at <www.engsc.ac.uk/er/theory/learning.asp>.

Howe, M. J. A. (1999) *A teacher's guide to the psychology of learning* (2nd edn), Oxford: Blackwell Publishers.

Hynes, D. (1986) Theory into practice, in J. R. Baird & I. J. Mitchell (Eds) *Improving the quality of teaching and learning. An Australian case study—the PEEL project* (pp. 21–32), Melbourne: Monash University Print Services.

Jarrell, R. (1964) *The bat-poet*, New York: Macmillan.

Jeppesen, P. (2002) Linking: A strategy for enhancing learning, in J. Loughran, I. Mitchell & J. Mitchell (Eds) *Learning from teacher research* (pp. 91–114), New York: Teachers College Press.

Korthagen, F. A. J., Kessels, J., Koster, B., Langerwarf, B. & Wubbels, T. (2001) *Linking practice and theory: The pedagogy of realistic teacher education*, Malhwah, NJ: Lawrence Erlbaum Associates.

Krause, K. L., Bochner, S. & Duchesne, S. (2003) *Educational psychology for learning and teaching*, Southbank, Victoria: Thomson.

Lancaster, G., Mitchell, I. with Berry, A., Corrigan, D., Keast, S. et al. (Eds) (2007) *Engaging students in secondary science: An ASISTM project*, Melbourne: PEEL Publishing.

Lortie, D. C. (1975) *Schoolteacher*, Chicago: Chicago University Press.

Loughran, J. J. (1996) *Developing reflective practice: Learning about teaching and learning through modelling*, London: Falmer Press.

——(2002) Effective reflective practice: In search of meaning in learning about teaching, *Journal of Teacher Education*, 53(1), (pp. 33–43).

——(2006) *Developing a pedagogy of teacher education: Understanding teaching and learning about teaching*, London: Routledge.

Loughran, J. J. & Berry, A. (Eds) (2006) *Looking into practice: Cases of science teaching and learning, Volume 1* (2nd edn), Melbourne: Monash University Print Services.

Loughran, J. J., Berry, A. & Mulhall, P. (2006) *Understanding and developing science teachers' pedagogical content knowledge*, Rotterdam: Sense Publishers.

Loughran, J. J. & Northfield, J. R. (1996) *Opening the classroom door: Teacher, researcher, learner*, London: Falmer Press.

Lovitt, C. & Clarke, D. (1998) *MCTP: Professional development package, activity bank, Volume 1*, Canberra: Curriculum Development Centre.

Lytle, S. & Cochran-Smith, M. (1991) Teacher research as a way of knowing, *Harvard Educational Review*, 62(4), (pp. 447–74).

Marton, F. & Saljo, R. (1976) On qualitative differences in learning I, Outcome and process, *British Journal of Educational Psychology*, 46, (pp. 4–11).

Mason, J. (2002) *Researching your own practice: The discipline of noticing*, London: RoutledgeFalmer.

McClintock Collective (1988) *Getting into gear: Gender inclusive teaching strategies*, ACT: Curriculum Development Centre.

Mitchell, I. (Ed.) (2007) *Teaching to reflect learning: The complete book of PEEL teaching procedures* (3rd edn), Melbourne: PEEL Publishing.

Mitchell, I. & Mitchell, J. (Eds) (1997) *Stories of reflective teaching: A book of PEEL cases*, Melbourne: PEEL Publishing.

Munby, H., Russell, T. & Martin, A. K. (2001) Teachers' knowledge and how it develops, in V. Richardson (Ed.) *Handbook of research on teaching* (4th edn, pp. 877–904), Washington DC: American Educational Research Association.

Myers, C. B. & Simpson, D. J. (1998) *Re-creating schools: Places where everyone learns and likes it*, Thousand Oaks, California: Corwin Press, Inc.

Novak, J. D. & Gowin, D. B. (1984) *Learning how to learn*, Cambridge: Cambridge University Press.

Osborne, R. J. & Freyburg, P. (Eds) (1985) *Learning in science: The implications of children's science*, Auckland: Heinemann.

Osler, J. & Flack, J. (2008) *Whose learning is it? Developing children as active and responsible learners*, Rotterdam: Sense Publishers.

Pfundt, H. & Duit, R. (2000) *Bibliography: Students' alternative frameworks and science education* (5th edn), Kiel, Germany: Institute of Science Education, University of Kiel.

Piaget, J. (1953) *Logic and psychology*, Manchester: Manchester University Press.

Pinnis, G. (2002) The L files: Motoring towards metacognition in the classroom, in J. Loughran, I. Mitchell & J. Mitchell (Eds) *Learning from teacher research* (pp. 152–70), New York: Teachers College Press.

Pintrich, P. R., Marx, R. W. & Boyle, R. A. (1993) Beyond cold conceptual change: The role of motivation beliefs and classroom contextual factors in the process of conceptual change, *Review of Educational Research*, 63, (pp. 167–99).

Rowe, E. (2008) Letting go, in J. Loughran & A. Berry (Eds) *Looking into practice: Cases of science teaching and learning (Volume 3)* (pp. 93–5), Melbourne: Monash University Print Services.

Rowe, M. B. (1974a) Wait-time and rewards as instructional variables, their influence on language, logic, and fate control: Part one: Wait-time, *Journal of Research in Science Teaching*, 11(2), (pp. 81–94).

——(1974b) Relation of wait-time and rewards to the development language, logic and fate control: Part two: Rewards, *Journal of Research in Science Teaching*, 11(4), (pp. 291–308).

Ryle, G. (1949) *The concept of mind*, London: Hutchinson.

Schön, D. A. (1983) *The reflective practitioner: How professionals think in action*, New York: Basic Books.

Senese, J. (2002) Opposites attract: What I learned about being a classroom teacher by being a teacher educator, in J. Loughran & T. Russell (Eds) *Improving teacher education practices through self-study* (pp. 43–55), London: RoutledgeFalmer.

Shulman, J. H. (1992) *Case methods in teacher education*, New York: Teachers College Press.

Shulman, L. S. (1986) Those who understand: Knowledge growth in teaching, *Educational Researcher*, 15(2), (pp. 4–14).

——(1999) Taking learning seriously, *Change*, 31(4), (pp. 10–17).

Stenhouse, L. (1975) *An introduction to curriculum research and development*, London: Heinemann.

Sternberg, R. J. (1985) *Beyond IQ: A triarchic theory of human intelligence*, New York: Cambridge University Press.

Swaim, J. (1998) In search of an honest response, *Language Arts*, 75(2), (pp. 118–25).

——(2004) In search of an honest response, in *Regarding children's words: Teacher research on language and literacy* (pp. 71–9), New York: Teachers College Press.

Swan, S. & White, R. T. (1994) *The thinking books*, London: Routledge.

Tobin, K. & Capie, W. (1980) The effects of teacher wait time and questioning quality on middle school science achievement, *Journal of Research in Science Teaching*, 17, (pp. 469–75).

van Manen, M. (1999) The language of pedagogy and primacy of student experience, in J. Loughran (Ed.) *Researching teaching: Methodologies and practices for understanding pedagogy* (pp. 13–27), London: Falmer Press.

von Glasersfeld, E. (1995) *Radical constructivism*, London: Falmer Press.

Vygotsky, L. (1962) *Thought and language*, Cambridge, MA: MIT Press, published originally in Russian in 1934.

White, R. T. (1988) *Learning science*, Oxford: Blackwell Publishers.

Whitehead, J. (1993) *The growth of educational knowledge: Creating your own living educational theories*, Bournemouth: Hyde Publications.

Zanting, A., Verloop, N. & Vermunt, J. D. (2003) How do student teachers elicit their mentor teachers' practical knowledge?, *Teachers and Teaching: Theory and Practice*, 9(3), (pp. 197–211).

Zeichner, K. M. (1995) Reflections of a teacher educator working for social change, in T. Russell & F. Korthagen (Eds), *Teachers who teach teachers* (pp. 11–24), London: Falmer Press.

Index

A
academic knowledge, 41
accomplished teacher, being an, x, xi,
159
action and intent, tension between, 52
active learning environment, 35, 106,
126, 168, 173, 181
activities that work, 48, 51, 20, *see also*
teaching procedures
affective component of learning, 63
alternative perspectives/frames, 24, 164,
210, 212
anecdotes, 40, 187–9
'apprenticeship of observation', *see*
Lortie, Dan
assessing own learning/student as
teacher, 153
assumptions, 9, 12, 50
atheoretical knowledge, 13, 41, 184
attitudes, 43, 57, 162
axioms to help understand practice, x

B
Baird, Cate, 165
Baird, John, 137, 144
behaviour(s), 3, 8, 176
    default, 5
beliefs, 12

Berry, Amanda, 14, 50–1, 54, 214,
215
Biggs, John, 61
blogs, 201–7
Bloom, Benjamin, 24–6, 43, 126
Boyle, Lynn, 137, 140
brainstorming, 71–2, 195–6, *see also*
teaching procedures
Brookfield, Stephen, 9
building up ideas, 58, 125
busyness of teaching, 4, 41, 212
Buzan, Tony, 102

C
cases methodology, 18
chunking, 27, 80, 86–7
classroom,
    actions ix, xi
    activities, *see* teaching procedures
    decision-making by students in the,
        148–9, 195, 197, 206, 207–8
    discussion 6, 95, 151–2, 196
    experience in the, 37, 41–2, 185,
        210
    interaction, 4–9, 15, 62, 204
    learning, 143–4
    management, 12, 22, 174–9, 180–6,
        213

classroom, *(Cont.)*
    practice, 41, 43–51, 82, 137,
        148,152, 166–7, 169–72, 186,
        190, 210
Cochran-Smith, Marilyn, 44, 185,
    217
cognitive development, 21
cognitive dissonance, 53, 62
cognitive strategies, 33, *see also* memory
collaboration, 5, 193, 212, 215–16
communication sheets, 174–5, 195, 197
complexity of teaching, 10, 218
concrete operational developmental
    stage, 20, *see also* Piaget, Jean
confidence, 4, 7, 14, 17–18, 30, 52–3,
    112, 123, 128, 170, 188, 198, 205,
    211
constructivism, 34–5
contour map, 118
CoRe, 45–7
craft knowledge, 45

D
DeBono, Edward, 43, 101–2
decision-making, by teachers, 11–13
deep and surface learning, 28–31, 80
default
    approach to learning, 29, 92, 94,
        106, 108
    behaviours, 7
Dewey, John, 42, 50, 161, 127, 162–5,
    205, 220

E
elements of memory, 31–4
emotional intelligence, 24
engaging students in learning, xi–xii,
    49, 107, 201, 206
environmental influence on
    intelligence, 22
episodes, 32, 43, 93–4, 114, *see also*
    memory
episteme, 186
experience,

role in shaping practice, 12, 14–5,
    34, 38, 40, 41–2, 44, 51, 53,
    163–5, 185, 187–8, 210, 218
role in student learning, 37–8, 92,
    94–5, 99, 107–8
experiment, letting students, 203
expertise,
    articulating, ix, 210,
    developing, 5, 7, 11, 14, 37–40, 47,
        54, 56, 163–4, 209, 212–13,
        218

F
feedback, 60, 142, 204
Fenstermacher, Gary, 41
formal operational developmental
    stage, 20, *see also* Piaget, Jean
framing, x, 7, 51, 164, 212
Freer, Liz, 119–23
Freire, Paulo, 36, 38
frustration, 53, 175, 177, 179, 194

G
Gardner, Howard, 23–4
generalisable knowledge, 42, 43, 58
genetic influence on intelligence, 22
Goleman, Daniel, 24
good learning behaviours (GLBs),
    145–6, 150–3
Gordon, W.J.J., 100–1
Grimmett, Peter, 45
'guess what's in the teacher's head', 6,
    61

H
Higher Education Academy
    Engineering Subject Centre
    (HEA), 29
higher-order thinking, 25–7, 123, 126,
    135
Hoban, Garry, 114, 221
Hynes, Damien, 146–8
hypothesis, 163

I
images, 32, *see also* memory
independence of students, 52, 108, 205, 207–9
intellectual skills, 32–3, *see also* memory
intelligence, 22–4
Intelligence Quotient (IQ), 22–3

J
Jeppesen, Pia, 194–5, 198
journal keeping
    students', 64
    teachers' 60, 165–8, 171, 180–1

K
knowing that, knowing how, 26
knowledge, 41–2
    articulating, 50
    for practice, 44, 46, 56
    in action, 44–5
    of practice, xi, 44, 210
    of teaching, 13
Korthagen, Fred, 13, 186

L
language of teaching and learning, 47, 124
learner's perspective, 15
learning, 58, 79
    artefacts, 134
    about oneself as a teacher, 179
    about the knowledge of practice, 209
    through experience, 38, 164
    through reflection on practice, 165
    to make the abstract concrete, 110
letting go, 16
linking, 80, 91 *see also* teaching procedures
    cycle, 97
    through a labelled diagram, 97

to real life, 99
very different parts of the work, 98
log book, 63–4
long-term memory, 27, 80
Lortie, Dan, 7
Loughran, John, 7, 11, 40, 45, 48, 59, 108, 113, 151–2, 162, 189, 206, 209, 220–222

M
management techniques, 177
Markus, Vojtech, 207–9
Marton, Ference, 20, 32
Mason, John, 15–16
Mathematics Curriculum Teaching Package (MCTP), 109
maths, 59, 166–9, 174–5, 179
McClintock Collective, 118
memory, 26, 80
mental ability, 21
metacognition, 4, 29, 102, 106, 142–3, 146, 148–50, 152–4, 157–8, 194, 220, 222
Milroy, Philippa, 50–1
misconceptions, 30, 62, 172, 194
Mitchell, Ian, 145
monitoring, 143, 153
Moody, Bree, 202–5
motivation, 165, 175, 180
motor skills, 33, *see also* memory
multiple intelligences, 23–4

N
Northfield, Jeff, 48, 50–1, 59, 107, 151, 209
noticing, 19
Novak, Joseph, 66
novices, 37

O
Opening the classroom door, 59
open-mindedness, 162, 205
Osler, Jo, 74, 88, 91, 148, 153, 158
ownership of learning, 204

P
PaP-eRs, 45
passive learning, 148
pedagogical
  content knowledge, 45
  experiences, 49
  expertise, 37
  intent, 141
  relationships, 40
  response, 205
  skills, 61
pedagogy, 1, 35–8, 42, 51, 54, 103, 107,
  146, 148, 166, 183–6, 209, 212–13,
  219, 221, 223
PEEL, 4, 98, 135, 143, 145–8, 220–2
personal experience, 75, 193
personal understanding, 42
phronesis, 186
Piaget, Jean, 20–22, 34
Pinnis, Gillian, 152–3
planning, 153
  for learning, 53
predicting, 126
preoperational developmental stage, 20
principles, 12–13, 34
  of teaching for quality learning, 107
prior knowledge, 57–8, 73, 106
  building on, 60
problem, 163
problematic nature of teaching, 13–14
procedural language, 191
processing, 3, 27–8, 78–80, 90
professional development, xii, 159,
  180–2, 200, 216
professional judgment, 15
professional knowledge, 1, 4, 44, 47–50,
  79, 82, 161, 181
  of practice, ix–xi, 1, 42, 50–5, 82,
    149, 165, 190, 193, 199, 212–16
  making explicit, 44
professional learning, xii, 4, 10, 15, 159,
  183, 200–1, 209, 211–12, 216, 220
professional practice, 56
professional satisfaction, 9

progress, 94
propositional knowledge, 79
propositions, 32, *see also* memory
psychology, 24, 79
public/codified knowledge, 41, 44

Q
quality learning, 49, 59
quality teaching, 218
questioning, 4–6, 61

R
rationalising behaviour, 7, 182, 214
reasoning, 163
recounting, 154
reflection, 14, 15, 33, 37–8, 48, 142,
  153, 161, 166, 181–3, 210
reflective
  account, 183
  journal, 64
  practitioners, 164
reframing, 5, 7, 10, 164, 212
relationships, 174
research, 61
  audience, 186
  questions, 185–6, 194
responding
  to students, 6
  to GLBs, 151
responsibility, 162
  for learning, 4, 170, 172, 174, 208,
    213
revisionary tasks, 192
risk taking, 5, 11, 40, 204
rote learn, 78
routines, school-learning, 108
routine tasks, 106
Rowe, Esther, 16
Rowe, Mary Budd, 8
Ryle, Gilbert, 26

S
safety, 52
scholarship, 49

in teaching, 56
Schön, Donald, 7, 14, 163
science of educating, 36
scientist's explanation, 58
'scripts', following, 34, 53, 60, 79, 80,
    94, 148, 191
selection, 27, *see also* reflection
self-
    study, 180–2, 215, 220, 223
    understanding and awareness, 214
sensorimotor developmental stage, 20,
    see also Piaget, Jean
sharing intellectual control, 107
short-term memory, 26
Shulman, Lee, 18, 45, 49
sociohistorical influences on learning,
    21
specialist knowledge, 42
specialised
    knowledge of practice, 43
    language, 48
Sternberg, Robert, 24
strings, 32, *see also* memory
structured thinking, 135
students' learning, 9
students' understanding
    development, 61
    enhancement, 33
Studies of Society and the
    Environment, 137
suggestions, 163, *see* Dewey, John
surface processing, 80
Swaim, Jim, 190, 192
Swan, Sue, 64, 100
synthesising, 125–141

T
teacher, 5
    as learner, 15, 37
    change preceding student change,
        49
    research, 4, 50, 184–7, 189–90,
        192–4, 196
    thinking, 13

professional knowledge of practice,
    ix, 19, 41–5, 54–5, 78, 148, 216
teaching and learning, xi
    episodes, 178
    for understanding, 82
    process, 182
    as problematic, 13, 161
teaching procedure(s), 37, 62
    analysing a picture/poster, 86
    anticipation reaction guide, 73–4
    Before before/after after, 132–3
    Before–Now–After, 132
    brainstorming, 71–2
    card sorting, 65–6
    concept map, 66–70
    constructing a list of good learning
        behaviours, 150–1
    continuum, 137–9
    creating analogies, 100
    creating headings/sub-headings, 84
    creating links, 218
    creative writing, 118
    design and create a learning
        artefact, 134
    fact file, 88
    fishbowl discussion, 135
    fortune lines, 114, 116
    Frayer model, 76
    from there to here, 96
    graphs into action, 119
    grids, 86–7
    how to read a poem, 136
    information grid, 85
    interpretive discussion, 156
    jigsaw groupwork method, 132
    jumbled text, 82–4
    Know–What–Learn–How
        (KWLH), 70–1
    knowing what type of thinking is
        needed, 154
    learning from discussion, 134
    letting the students decide the
        content, 207
    L-files, 152–3

teaching procedure(s) *(Cont.)*
   linking cycle, 97
   linking through a labelled diagram,
     97
   linking to real life, 99
   linking very different parts of the
     work, 98–9
   list of procedures, 153–4
   mind maps, 102–3
   model making, 116–18
   moving-on map, 157–8
   Plus–Minus–Interesting (PMI),
     89–90
   Predict–Observe–Explain (POE),
     149–50
   postbox, 133–4
   probe of prior views, 62
   question dice, 85–6
   question grid, 84
   recounting, 154
   responding to good learning
     behaviours, 151–2
   role play, 110–13
   self-assessed learning, 153
   semantic map, 74–5
   slowmation, 114
   story from a graph/graph from a
     story, 108–9
   storyboarding (text to pictures), 113
   structured thinking, 135–6
   Suchman technique, 128–30
   summary reflective writing, 63–5
   Sweller questions, 100
   synectics, 100–1
   T-cards, 194, 196
   thinking books, 64, 194, 196, 197,
     223
   thinking hats, 101–2
   Think–Pair–Share, 72
   topic linkup, 194, 196
   Venn diagrams, 156
   What can you work out?, 130–1
   What if . . .?, 95
   Write your own method, 119
   Writing a song or a poem, 118–19
   Writing on the reading, 88–9
teaching, 3
   profession, 181
   technical, 4
telling, 52
tensions, 51
testing, 163
theory/theoretical, 43
   explanation, 43
   perspectives, 48
theory–practice gap, 13, 31, 41–2, 48,
   54, 161, 184, 186
thinking processes, 127
transformation, education as, 36
translation, 104, 106
triarchic model of intelligence, 24
trusting students as learners, 213
uncertainty, 39
uncommunicative students, 177
understanding, 10
   of teaching, 12, 212

V
van Manen, Max, 36, 187
von Glasersfeld, Ernst, 34
Vygotsky, Lev, 21, 22, 34

W
wait time, 8, 10, *see also* questioning
Weschler Intelligence Scales, 22
'what's in the teacher's head', 6, 61,
   207, 208
White, Richard, 31, 81, 105
Whitehead, Jack, 214
whole-heartedness, 162
withholding judgement, 6, 61, 202,
   204, 205, 209

Z
zone of proximal development (ZPD),
   21